Living Free Even Financially

Discover the secrets of true enrichment

Rudi Louw

Many Scripture quotations are taken from the *Revised Standard Version*, Holy Bible, Thomas Nelson Publishers. Copyright © 1983 by Thomas Nelson, Inc.

Some Scripture quotations were taken from the *New King James Version*, Holy Bible, Thomas Nelson Publishers. Copyright © 1983 by Thomas Nelson, Inc.

All Scripture quotations not taken from the RSV, NKJV and the Mirror Bible are a literal translation of the Scriptures.

The Holy Scriptures are just that; HOLY.

Statements enclosed in brackets were inserted into Scripture quotations *to add emphasis or to clarify the meaning of what is being said in those scriptures.* **The integrity of God's Word to man was not compromised in any way. Due care and diligence was cautiously exercised to keep the Word of Truth intact.**

For example: The apostle Paul said in his second letter to Timothy in chapter three verse sixteen that:

"All Scripture is given by inspiration of God (literally God breathed), *and is profitable for doctrine, for reproof, for correction, for instruction **in righteousness**."* NKJV

2

Content

The marvel of the Holy Bible

1. The *theme* and *inspired thought* of Scripture continue *uninterrupted.*

It took *1500 years* to compile the Holy Bible, involving *more than 40 different authors*, yet the theme and inspired thought of Scripture continues *uninterrupted*, from author to author, from beginning till end.

2. Absence of *mythical stories:*

Compare philosophies and theories about creation in the Middle East, Europe, Asia, Africa and Latin America, and you'll find mythical scenarios, gods feuding and cutting up other gods to form the heavens and the earth. In ancient Greek mythology, the Greeks see Atlas carrying the earth on his shoulders. In India, Hindus believe 8 elephants carry the earth on their backs.

But in contrast, Job, the oldest book in the Holy Bible, declares that *God suspends the earth 'on nothing.'* (Job 26:7)

This was said millennia before Isaac Newton discovered the invisible laws of gravity that delicately balance every planet and sun in its individual circuit.

In contrast to every other ancient attempt to give a creation account, *the Holy Bible pictures the creation of the earth in a very scientific manner.*

In Gen 1 for instance, the continents are lifted from the seas, then vegetation is created and later, animal life, all reproducing *'according to its own kind,'* **thus recognising the fixed genetic laws.**

Finally we have the creation of man and woman, *all done by God in a dignified and proper manner, without mythological adornments.*

The rest of the Holy Bible follows suite.

The narratives are **true historical documents,** *faithfully reflecting society and culture,* **as history and archaeology would discover them thousands of years later. Not only is the Holy Bible historically accurate, it is also reliable when it deals with scientific subjects.**

It was not written as a textbook on history, science, mathematics or medicine, *yet,* **when its writers touch on these subjects, they often state facts that scientific**

advancement would not reveal or even consider until thousands of years later.

While many have doubted the accuracy of the Holy Bible, time and continued research have consistently demonstrated that the Word of God is better informed than its critics.

3. The Holy Bible is *intact*.

Of all the ancient works of substantial size, the Holy Bible against all odds and expectations survives intact.

Compared with other ancient writings, the Holy Bible has more manuscripts as evidence to support it than any ten pieces of classical literature combined!

The plays of William Shakespeare, for instance, were written about four hundred years ago, and written after the invention of the printing press.

Many of his original words have been lost in numerous sections, *yet the Holy Bible's uncanny preservation has weathered thousands of years of wars, contradictions, persecutions, fires and invasions. Jewish scribes,* **like no other manuscript has ever been preserved**, *preserved the Holy Bible's Old Covenant text through centuries.*

They kept tabs on every letter, syllable, word and paragraph.

*They continued from generation to generation to appoint and train special classes of men within their culture **whose sole duty it was to preserve and transmit these documents <u>with perfect accuracy and fidelity</u>.***

Who ever bothered to count the letters, syllables, or words of Plato, Aristotle or Seneca for that matter?

When it comes to the New Testament, the actual number of preserved manuscripts is so great that it becomes overwhelming.

There are more than 5,680 Greek manuscripts, more than 10,000 Latin Vulgate and at least 9,300 other versions; there exist a further 25,000 manuscript copies of portions of the New Testament.

No other document of antiquity even begins to approach such numbers.

The closest in comparison is Homer's <u>Iliad</u> with only 643 manuscripts. The first complete work of Homer only dates back to the 13th century.

4. In dealing with time, the Holy Bible *accurately foretells what will*

happen ahead of time with unmatched results.

No other ancient work even begins to attempt this.

Other books claim divine inspiration, such as the Koran, the Book of Mormon, and parts of the Veda. *But none of these books contains predictive foretelling.*

This one fact we know for certain, and it is undeniable: *While microscopic scrutiny would show up the imperfections, blemishes and defects of any work of man, <u>it magnifies the beauties and perfection of God</u>, just as every flower displays in accurate detail, the reflection and perfection of beauty, <u>so does the Word of Truth when it is scrutinized</u>.*

Historian, Philip Schaff wrote:

'...Without money and weapons, Jesus the Christ conquered more millions, than Alexander, Caesar, Mohammed and Napoleon. Without science and learning, He (Jesus the Christ) shed more light on things human and divine than all philosophers and scholars combined. Without the eloquence of schools, He (Jesus the Christ) spoke such words of life as was never spoken before or since and produced effects, which lie beyond the reach of orator or poet. Without writing a single line, He

*(Jesus the Christ) set more pens in motion, and furnished themes for more sermons, orations, discussions, learned volumes, works of art, and songs of praise, **than the whole army of great men of ancient and modern times combined.**'* (The person of Christ, p33. 1913)

Today, there are literally billions of Bibles in more than 2,000 languages, *isn't it about time you find out what it really has to say?* Hey listen, the Holy Bible is all about Jesus, the Messiah, the Christ *...and everything about Jesus Christ is really about YOU!!*

Study tips:

Read 2 Corinthians 5:14, 16, 18, 19, and 21. In the light of these scriptures it should be obvious that if you want to study the Holy Bible *you should study it in the light of mankind's Redemption!*

Daily feed on Redemption Realities, especially Romans 1 through 8, Ephesians, Colossians, Galatians, 1 Peter 1, 2 Peter 1, James 1, 1 and 2 Corinthians, and the book of Acts.

Acknowledgement

I want to acknowledge and thank one of my mentors in the faith, Francois du Toit, for blessing and impacting my life with revelation knowledge.

The portion on *"The marvel of the Holy Bible"* was borrowed from his website: http://www.mirrorword.net/ as students so often feel they have a right to do with things that come from teachers they respect.

Just as Galatians 6:6 says:

*"Let him who is taught the Word **share in all good things** with him who teaches."*

To all our other many dear friends and family, and all those who helped me with this project,

…but especially to my sweet wife Carmen:

For all your love and support,

THANK YOU!

Foreword

Thank you for taking the time to read this book.

Let me start off by saying that I am totally addicted to my Daddy's love for me; I am in love with Jesus Christ, *and that is enough for me!*

The love of God is so much more than a doctrine, a philosophy, or a theory; it is so much more and goes so much deeper than knowledge; it way surpasses knowledge, *we are talking heart language here,*

…therefore this book was not written to impress intellectuals with knowledge and philosophy, theologians with theories and doctrine, nor English majors with grammar and spelling for that matter,

…so if you come up with any other definitions or find any language inaccuracies please don't use it to disqualify Love's own message I bring to you in this book.

I write *to impact people's hearts;*

…to make them see the mysteries that has been hidden in Father God's heart, concerning Christ Jesus, and really *concerning THEM,* so as to arrest their conscience with it, *that I may introduce them to their original design, and to their true selves;* **and present them to themselves perfect in Christ Jesus and set them apart unto Him in love**, as a chaste virgin,

"...for by Him all things were created... All things were created through Him and for Him. And He is before all things

(He has been in existence from the beginning, He has always been in existence, and holds the place of preeminence over everything; He is the Prince of LIFE Himself), *and in Him all things consist"* - Colossians 1:16 & 17

Everything in creation is still working according to its design and is held together in Him; in His power proceeding from His heart of love. Everything and everyone finds their place of existence; their function and purpose; their place of significance; their very reason for being; their very home and belonging, in Him who loves them and gave Himself to them

We are involved with the biggest romance of the ages;

...therefore this book cannot be read as you would a novel; casually. It is not a cleverly devised little myth or fable.

It contains revelation and *truth* into some things you may or may not have considered before. It is not blasphemy or error though.

14

It is the TRUTH of God, ultimate TRUTH, and therefore has direct bearing upon YOUR life,

…**the Word and the Spirit is my witness** *to the reality of these things!*

Be like the people of Berea the apostle Paul ministered to in Acts 17:11. *Open yourself up to study the revelation contained in this book,*

…but be forewarned, do not become guilty of the sins of the Pharisees, **or you too will miss out on the depth of fulfillment God Himself, who is LOVE, wants to give you**.

(Jesus said of the Pharisees and Sadducees that they strain out every little gnat BUT swallow whole camels. What He meant by that is that *some people seem to have it all together when it comes to doctrine and they love to argue. It makes them feel important,*

…*but it is nothing other than EMPTY religious and intellectual pride. They know the Scriptures in and out, and YET they are still so IGNORANT about REAL TRUTH that is only found in LOVE; they are indifferent towards the things that REALLY MATTERS.*

They always argue over the use of every little jot and tittle and over the meaning and interpretation of every word of Scripture.

The exact thing they accuse everyone else of doing though; the precise thing they judge everyone else for, they end up actually doing themselves, that is:

…they often completely misinterpret and twist what is being said, making a big deal of insignificant things, *while obscuring or weakening God's real truth; the truth of His LOVE.*

They always major on minors, **because they do not understand the heart of God**

…**and** *therefore they constantly miss the whole point of the message*.)

Paul himself said it so beautifully:

"…*the letter kills but* **the Spirit BRINGS LIFE;**"

"…*knowledge puffs up, but* **LOVE EDIFIES**."

I say again:

Allow yourself to get caught up in the revelation I am about to share. Open yourself up to study the insight contained in this book *not only with a desire to gain knowledge, but also* **with anticipation** *to hear from Father God yourself;*

…**to encounter Him through His Word; and to embrace truth,**

...in order to know and believe the LOVE God has for <u>you</u>, and to get so caught up in it, that you too may receive from Him; LOVES' impartation of LIFE.

This revelation contains within it the voice and call of LOVE Himself to every human being on the face of this earth.

If you take heed to it, it is custom designed and guaranteed to forever alter and enrich your life!

"I have come
that you may have **life**
and have **it** more abundantly."

"For God is able
to make all grace abound toward
you,
that you,
always having all sufficiency in
all things,
may have an abundance for
every good work."

"He who supplies seed to the
sower

and bread for food
will supply and multiply your
resources..."

"You will be enriched in every
way
for great liberality and
generosity."

John 10:10;
2Corintians 9:8, 10~11

Prayer

As we come to You right now, Father, we thank you that we may bring honor and glory to You.

Father we thank you that we may respond to Your initiative.

And as we love You right now Father, *our love has become a reflection of Your love towards us.*

So, *we do not feel inferior* in our loving You.

Father *we are conscious of the abundance of the love You have for us that is shed abroad in our hearts* as we give expression of our hearts in our praise and in our adoration to You who alone are worthy.

Father, we are so thankful.

We thank you for Your precious living word, for its eternal influence; its eternal impact in our lives.

And as we explore Your word we are conscious of the Holy Spirit's unction; of Him who enlightens our understanding; of Him who leads us into all TRUTH.

And so, we honor You by being sensitive to You as our teacher, Holy Spirit.

Thank you for teaching us all that the Father wants us to know, the deep things of His heart and of His Kingdom.

In Jesus Name

Amen

Chapter 1

A corrupt system

In this book I want to address *a most important subject.*

It has to do with **what you believe** *and* **how you live your life**, and as you can already conclude from the title, *it will affect your finances.*

I believe it is very vitally important for every single one of us *to grasp these concepts I am about to share with you in this book,*

…**because none of the governmental systems of this world, secular or religious,** *have ever been able to develop a monitory system that does not enslave the best of us to corrupt values.*

I believe the secrets to true enrichment and true fulfillment I am about to share with you has the potential *to elevate you to a new place spiritually as far as your finances are concerned;*

…*a place of such freedom and abundance;*

...a place where the governmental systems of this world, through their monetary systems have been unable to take you!

I truly believe that we can all live *unrestricted lives;*

...we can all enjoy such *liberality of heart;*

...we can have *such **a release of abundance in our spirit** that we would come to the point in our lives of **contentment in all things**.*

I am talking about **having an abundance** *for every one of the good works we want to accomplish.*

I'm talking about **experiencing the measure of abundance Jesus Christ talked about,**

John 10:10

10 *"I have come **to give you** **life** and that you may have **it** **more abundantly**."*

If we as individuals *can grasp* the principles of the law of enrichment; of the law of faith and of the law of love, *and begin to walk in it,*

...then I believe we will escape the corruption that is running more and more rampant in the world *through lust,*

...and we will enter into a life *of such **liberality of heart; a truly unrestricted abundant life!***

I say again:

If we grasp these things and begin to walk in them, *a very powerful force will be released in our lives and in our finances,*

...a force that brings about,

Luke 6:38

38 *"...**good measure, pressed down, shaken together and running over.***"

Just think of how powerful the laws that govern aviation are; *these forces are stronger than the law of gravity,* and we know how strong a force gravity is.

Well, the law of true enrichment and true fulfillment is every bit as powerful as any other laws that govern the universe, and **when this law of true enrichment and true fulfillment is activated in your life, *it affects your finances;***

...*an abundance will be released for every good work.*

I want us to discover *the principle* that God wants to release to us *through His Word; the principle that God desires to **activate in us**,*

...to enable us to live *above the systems of this world* when it comes to finances

You don't have to search far to see that **one of the most successful methods the enemy has used** *to diminish the light of the Christian Church, and to ruin our witness in this world, **is corruption as far as finances is concerned.***

It is sad to say, but, *many in the Christian Church* **have sold themselves to a corrupt system.**

I say again:

I really believe that *the devil has deceived most Christian leaders in the body of Christ,*

...*to sell themselves to a corrupt system,*

...*especially as far as finances are concerned.*

They have ruined *the kind of purity of heart <u>God desires His leaders, us, to have</u> before all men.*

You see, there is a certain quality of purity of heart God desires for us to walk in when it comes to the area of finances,

...*that we can no longer afford to fall short of,*

...*if we want to be vessels <u>ready for Masters' use</u> in His great harvest.*

It is quite amazing to see, **how successfully the enemy has been able to use many of God's ministers,**

…through the area of finances,

…to again undo all the good things in people's hearts and lives,

…that God initially imparted to them through us, His ministers.

I mean, through his clever strategy of deception in the area of finances *the enemy has had to do almost nothing,*

…we ourselves often undo the very work God has begun through us in people's lives.

Listen, *the enemy has enjoyed enough success in this area,* **it is time we put him in his place, under our feet where he belongs!**

I want us to discover from the Scriptures the principle **that releases us in our personal experience** *to live above the strategies of the enemy.*

Let's turn to Matthew 6 to begin with.

Now every time we hear Jesus saying something *that sounds very irresponsible to the natural mind,*

...we need to evaluate what Jesus says in terms of His provision,

...and in terms of His person, who He is, *His love for us, and His character,*

...in terms of the integrity of His Word, *in terms of His covenant with us,*

...and in terms of the truth of His Word, *in terms of faith,*

...and in terms of *love!*

Chapter 2

Anxiety the root of greed

Matthew 6:19-21, 25-34

19 *"Do not lay up for yourselves treasure on earth where moth and rust consumes and where thieves break in and steal,"*

20 *"…but lay up for yourselves treasure in heaven where neither moth nor rust consumes and where thieves do not break in and steal."*

21 *"For where your treasure is, there your heart will be also"*

25 *"I tell you, do not be anxious about your life what you shall eat, or what you shall drink, nor about your body what you shall put on. Is not life more than food and the body more than clothing?"*

26 *"Look at the birds of the air, they neither sow, nor reap, nor gather into barns and yet **your** Heavenly Father feeds them. **Are you not of more value to Him than they?**"*

27 *"Can any of you through anxiety add a single hour to your span of life?"*

28 *"Why are you anxious about clothing? Consider the flowers of the fields; they neither toil nor spin"*

29 *"…yet I tell you, even Solomon in all his glory was not arrayed like one of these."*

30 *"If God so clothes the grass of the fields which is alive today and dead tomorrow and can be thrown into the oven,* **will He not much more clothe you, O you of little faith?***"*

31 *"Therefore do not be anxious saying: 'What shall we eat?' or 'What shall we drink?' or 'What shall we wear?'*

32 *"For the gentiles* **seek** *all these things; indeed* **your** *Heavenly Father* **knows that you need all these things***"*

33 *"But seek first* (as your highest priority; exclusively) *the righteousness of God and His Kingdom…*

(He is talking about your spirit identity, about His indwelling in your spirit – the kingdom of God is about knowing your righteousness, it's about peace and joy in the Holy Spirit)

"But seek first (as your highest priority; exclusively) *the righteousness of God and His Kingdom (within you – the reign of His Spirit; of His truth, and of His peace and of His joy within you)…***and all these things shall be added unto you.***"*

34 *"Therefore do not be anxious about tomorrow…"*

Matthew 6:25

25 *"I tell you, do not be anxious about your life…"*

The King James version says:

25 *"I say unto you, **take no thought** for your life…"*

*"…**take no thought**…"*

*"…**do not be anxious** about your life…"*

Anxiety usually begins through meditating upon negative things.

Perhaps not even negative things, *but things that concern you* …things that take your attention away from the things at hand,

…those concerns you mull over in your spirit that takes your attention away from priorities you should be busy with, priorities that need your immediate attention *and focus.*

It is a fact that we would be a lot better at things and get a lot more accomplished *if we would just stop worrying,*

…if we would just stop stressing!

Matthew 6:25

*"...**take no thought**..."* or *"...**do not be anxious** about your life, what you shall eat, or what you shall drink, nor about your body, what you shall put on..."*

If just any person tells you to *"not be anxious about your life, what you shall eat, or what you shall drink,"*

...or if they tell you to *"...**take no thought**..."* **and you believe them and want to follow their advice and do what they say,** *you might as well prepare for your soon coming funeral,*

...because *"what you're going to eat,"* **and** *"what you're going to drink,"* **and** *"what you're going to put on"* **speaks of the most basic of our responsibilities in life.**

But when JESUS says this, *He is not just any man,*

...when JESUS says this, *He speaks from covenant knowledge.*

I mean when JESUS says this, *He knows what He is talking about.*

When JESUS says this, *it is spoken from an understanding that this thing called 'stress' drains our energy.*

*...*He knows that this anxiety, this thing called *'worry'* has become <u>*such a priority to us*</u> *that it has eclipsed our lives*,

*...*it dominates our entire lives; *it molds and determines our way of living; our lifestyle,*

...and it overrules our hearts constantly,

*...*and it obscures covenant knowledge!

And so He asks a question:

25 *"...Is not life more than food and the body more than clothing?"*

26 *"Look at the birds of the air, they neither sow, nor reap, nor gather into barns **and yet your Heavenly Father feeds them**..."*

Mankind as a whole, as far back as the first societies of people, generation after generation discovered,

(...and today it has become even more pronounced in our modern day and age, in our modern society,)

...we have all discovered these anxiety driven stress things, these systems we set up for ourselves, to cope with life and to become supposedly successful in life, and we have learned to live by it,

…we have learned that, through just a little bit of sowing (just a little investment)

…and *then through* **fully exploiting** *the principle of harvest, and the principle of gathering together into barns* **we can so develop our financial resources,**

…and we can become extremely wealthy in terms of worldly standards,

…and so we have pursued it!

But Jesus knows that **this concern of man, this anxiety, this stress, <u>this greed</u> is a deception!**

…and it has become **such an anxiety, such a stress,** in every generation,

…and especially in ours,

…that it totally <u>rules over our whole being</u>.

It has become *a source of alternative fulfillment,*

…an <u>alternate</u> source, an <u>alternate</u> lifestyle, an <u>alternate</u> fulfillment,

…to a being whom God created, and brought forth into this world <u>for a different purpose</u>!

But in our blindness we run head long over that anxiety and worry cliff, over that stress cliff and over that greed cliff,

...and we don't care *whether God made us for a different purpose or not,*

...*our whole being has so totally been contaminated and consumed* by this concern of ours, this anxiety, this stress, this greed that we find our fulfillment in life in,

...*our whole being has been so totally corrupted and consumed* in the principle of sowing and reaping

...*in sowing, yes, but especially reaping...in big time harvesting, and in gathering together into barns,*

...*our whole being has been so totally corrupted and consumed* in being anxious about *'What am I going to eat?' 'What am I going to drink?' 'What am I going to wear?'*

We are doing all this *just to feed the flesh!*

...*but it never really satisfies or fulfills.*

Listen, God has designed us and destined us *for a life* much larger *than just survival in the flesh.*

That is why Jesus decided to address this issue, *for in our anxiety about these things* <u>*we chase after insatiable cravings;*</u> <u>*insatiable greed,*</u>

…**and we miss out on** <u>**life**</u>**!**

Matthew 6:25

25 *"Is not life more than food and clothing?"*

You can go and speak to any professional businessman or women today *who are not walking in covenant relationship with God and in the Truth of the Word,*

…**and you'll find a person who lives an unfulfilled life to one degree or another.**

Their life does not fulfill them,

…they are constantly running *from one thing to another,*

…constantly running *after the next thing and the next thing and the next thing,*

…*only to find out* **they need something else in their life,**

…**for what they have does not fulfill them!**

Let me tell you something; *it can never fulfill them!*

…God did not design them to be fulfilled by those things.

Let's return to what Jesus has to say:

Matthew 6:26

26 *"Look at the birds of the air, they neither sow, nor reap, nor gather into barns **and yet your Heavenly Father feeds them. <u>Are you not of more value to Him than they</u>**?"*

If your Heavenly Father has so engineered and ordained the lifestyle of a little bird that, that little bird is not just born to die tomorrow, *but to live its life within an environment of ample provision,*

…*how much more will your Father's concern and care be towards you?*

I read in an article one day that the current wealth of the two wealthiest men of our age (worth billions of US Dollars), *combined with all their future earning potential,* (…now we are really talking Trillions of US Dollars here),

…all of their wealth put together, **would not be able to feed an eighth of the animal world for one day**.

Did you get that?

It will take *all their combined resources <u>of their lifetime</u>* **to feed** *merely an eighth* of the animal world, ***just for one single day!***

If you go to the national zoo in Washington DC or even just your local zoo, and just kind of take a look at their grocery list,

…it will release you from any anxiety for your own kitchen,

…even if you are responsible for running a soup kitchen, orphanage or Bible School!

Ha… ha… ha…

I mean if you see what they have to get together to feed those elephants and monkeys, and the kangaroos and giraffes and whatever they have in their cages over there, ***you will be amazed and released from anxiety all at the same time***.

Here in Matthew 6 **God says that *He* has taken responsibility to feed the birds.**

In Psalms 84:3 we read:

"Even the swallow finds a place where she may lay her young, at thy altars O Lord"

You see, when we too *discover the Lord to be our dwelling place, our provision, our sustenance* …we get liberated from any anxiety financially.

38

Chapter 3

Qualities that are highly esteemed

Financially speaking, much of what we call wisdom in this world we live in today *has been driven by nothing other than fear, anxiety and greed.*

Our wisdom has become *our own cage* of legalistic restrictions,

...and it has cramped us into a narrow place of existence;

...*literally robbed us of the spirit of <u>liberality</u> and <u>generosity</u> that we received from God.*

Don't be driven by fear, anxiety and greed and call it *the wisdom of God.*

Many times we talk about being responsible financially, *but we are talking out of our anxiety or greed.*

We do not even realize that we are merely emphasizing *the wisdom of this world.*

This kind of wisdom is earthly *and even demonic*,

…it robs you of your liberty!

…and leads to nothing but bondage!

Let me quote one of Jesus' parables *where He spoke about* **financial responsibility** and about **using money wisely.**

Luke 16:1-15

1 *"And He said to His disciples: "There was a certain rich man who had a steward, and an accusation was brought to him that this man was wasting and squandering his goods"*

2 *"So he called him and said to him, 'What is this I hear about you? Give an account of your stewardship, for you can no longer be steward.'*

3 *"Then the steward said within himself: 'What shall I do? For my master is taking the stewardship away from me. I cannot dig; I am ashamed to beg."*

4 *"I have resolved what to do, that when I am put out of the stewardship, they may receive me into their houses'*

5 *"So he called every one of his master's debtors to him, and said to the first: 'How much do you owe my master?'*

6 *"And he said: 'A hundred measures of oil.' So he said to him: 'Take your bill, and sit down quickly and write fifty.'*

7 *"Then he said to another: 'And how much do you owe?' So he said: 'A hundred measures of wheat.' And he said to him: 'Take your bill and write eighty.'*

8 **"So the master commended the unjust steward because he had dealt shrewdly.***"*

"For the sons of this world are more shrewd in their generation than the sons of light."

9 **"And I say to you, make friends for yourselves by** *(or by the use of)* *unrighteous mammon, so that,* **when** *it fails, they may receive you into everlasting habitations."*

10 *"He who is faithful **in what is least** is faithful also in much, and he who is unjust **in what is least** is unjust also in what is much."*

11 *"Therefore, **if you have not been faithful in the unrighteous mammon**, who will commit to your trust the true riches?"*

12 *"And if you have not been faithful, in what is another man's, who will give you what is your own?"*

13 **"No servant can serve two masters; for either he will hate the one, and love the other, or else he will be loyal to the one,**

and despise the other. You cannot serve God and mammon."

14 *"Now the Pharisees, **who were lovers of money**, also heard all these things, **and they turned up their noses at Him**"*

15 *"**But He said to them: 'You are those who <u>justify yourselves</u> before men, <u>but God knows your hearts</u>**."*

*"**For <u>what is highly esteemed</u> among men <u>is an abomination</u> in the sight of God.**"*

(If you look deeper you will see that Jesus not only spoke about financial responsibility and using money wisely, as far as God's perspective is concerned, *but He also took issue over not walking in mercy and forgiveness.*

He was speaking out against legalism among God's people, and how loading condemnation on people spiritually for missing the mark, *does not help relationships.*

He wasn't speaking about being politically correct either, giving license to sin, *kind of just accepting the person and the sin.*

No,

He was saying that *there are better ways* to get someone to stop missing the mark.)

Let's read it again and take a closer look at what He had to say about *financial responsibility* and about *using money wisely as far as God is concerned:*

Luke 16:1-15

1 *"And He said to His disciples: "There was a certain rich man who had a steward, and an accusation was brought to him that* **this man was wasting and squandering his goods**"

In other words, the man was financially irresponsible <u>according to the standards of this world</u>.

He was generous and kind to people and gave them ample grace and mercy.

On the surface it looked like it was *too much* grace and mercy, and that *he was allowing people to get away with too much.*

…It looked like he was *squandering* his master's goods, and *not being strict enough and hard enough,* on the so-called: "*debtors."*

2 *"So he* (the master) *called him and said to him, 'What is this I hear about you?* **Give an account of your stewardship**, *for you can no longer be steward.'*

3 *"Then the steward said within himself: 'What shall I do? For my master is taking the*

stewardship away from me. I cannot dig; I am ashamed to beg.'"

If you read it carefully, you will understand that Jesus was also speaking to the Pharisees, **who were wise according to the wisdom of this world,**

*…***but irresponsible** according to God*;

*…***they were not wise in God's eyes, when it came to God's work.**

4 '**I have resolved what to do,** *that when I am put out of the stewardship,* **they may receive me into their houses**'

5 *"So he called every one of his master's debtors to him, and said to the first: 'How much do you owe my master?'*

6 *"And he said, '***A hundred** *measures of oil.' So he said to him, 'Take your bill, and sit down quickly and write* **fifty***.'*

He actually forgave them a considerable portion of their debt; *up to 50%.*

So He was kind and generous towards them before,

*…***and now instead of repenting and getting harsh with them,**

*…***he is even more generous and kind**.

44

7 *"Then He said to another: 'And how much do you owe?' So he said, '**A hundred** measures of wheat.' And he said to him, 'Take your bill and write **eighty**.'*

Listen, this may not be *the wisdom of the business world,*

...but this was brilliant wisdom never-the-less, <u>Kingdom wisdom</u>.

It looked like he was wasting goods, *his master's goods,*

...*it wasn't his to waist; *it was his master's goods,

***...*he really *had no right to waste it,* being only a steward of it,**

***...*but he was wasting it none the less,**

...or was he really?

Let's consider what he *was really doing.*

He wasn't actually stealing it, hoarding it and spending it on himself and his own selfish desires,

No.

Through his actions he was using those goods *to not only build relationships with*

these people and win over their hearts in friendship,

…but he was also making friends <u>for his master</u> and making <u>his master's name</u> great

…and making <u>his master's</u> influence and business grow.

I think those legalistic fellow servants who accused him before his master were just jealous,

…like the Pharisees were towards Jesus

They could not understand *his unconventional ways,*

…His Kingdom Wisdom.

Now listen to how the master responded,

…and I do not believe for one moment that the master was a man who was just so easily fooled;

I do not believe that the master *was deceived, and had the wool pulled over his eyes by **any** of his servants.*

8 "**So the master commended the <u>unjust steward</u>…**"

Meaning the steward only **appeared** *irresponsible.*

46

It never ceases to amaze me that those who think outside of the box; those who are not bound by legalism, *but learn to unlock the love and the creativity inside of them,*

…are almost always judged by others, the legalistic ones,

*…**they are judged as rebels, lawbreakers or irresponsible people.***

"*…**He <u>commended</u> the** unjust **steward <u>because he had dealt shrewdly</u>**"

(He was operating in wisdom, *just a different wisdom*)

*"**For the sons of this world are shrewder in their generation than the sons of light**."*

Quite often, the sons of this world find it easier to think outside of the box, *because they are not bound by our legalistic religious rules.*

Also, there are sometimes more mercy and kindness shown by the average man in the street, *that doesn't even know God,* than in our legalistic religious circles.

The wisdom of thinking outside of our conventional boxes *can go a long way,*

…and so can, showing mercy and kindness towards *"debtors,"* or sinners.

I want you to take notice, and I emphasize again that, *it would have been wrong for this man* to waste his master's goods entrusted to him, *on himself,*

...but it was wisdom to *"waste"* goods in kindness to others, *in order to build relationships and win peoples hearts.*

It benefited the kingdom, *and in our case it will benefit the Kingdom of God and the work of the ministry.*

9 *"And I say to you, make friends for yourselves by* (or by the use of) *unrighteous mammon*

(Another translation says: *"by unrighteous wealth"*),

"...so that when it fails..."

(...when you run out of money or resources, or when you need help),

"...they"

(...the people whose hearts you won through kindness and generosity),

"...may receive you into everlasting habitations."

He was talking about being welcomed into their hearts and into their spirit.

Some say that he could be referring here to being awarded by God with *eternal **life** ...with **everlasting** habitations.*

That works for me too,

Our natural life and *what is truly spiritual* is quite often *much more connected than what we like to believe.*

...although I don't really think it was meant to be read and interpreted that way!

Ha... ha... ha...

He continues to say in verse 10,

10 *"He who is faithful..."*

Obviously not talking about faithfulness *in terms of how we usually view faithfulness*

10 *"He who is faithful **in what is least**..."*

People's souls are more important than money and things any day.

The faithfulness He is talking about is *being faithful in building relationships,*

...using money and earthly possessions *wisely, as a tool,*

...that means, *using it in liberality and generosity,*

...and so <u>winning people's hearts genuinely</u>.

10 *"He who is faithful in what is least..."*

"...is considered faithful also in much;"

"...and he who is unjust in what is least, he is (will be; shall be) unjust also in what is much."

We point fingers *at others,*

...but often we cannot guarantee *that we will not act the same way they do* **given the same set of circumstances**.

An unjust scale is an abomination in God's eyes.

The only problem is that **what God views as unjust,**

...and what we view as unjust,

...is not necessarily the same thing.

The wisdom of God *looks like foolishness* to man,

...and the wisdom of man is quite often *complete and utter foolishness as far as God is concerned.*

11 *"Therefore, if you have not been faithful* (**according to God's standards, not**

according to the so called wisdom of this world) *in the unrighteous mammon,"*

"…who will commit to your trust <u>the true riches</u>?"

This is a very real issue facing the Church today.

We have not been faithful *according to the wisdom of God,*

…**and it affects who we are as a person,** *in life and in ministry,*

…**it affects our unity and oneness of heart,** *with God and with one another,*

…**and our impact and effectiveness in this** *world,*

…**so how can we expect to see the power of God in the Church today like it was seen in the early Church, in the book of Acts?**

Or in other words,

"Who will commit to our trust <u>the true riches</u>?"

Proverbs 11:30

30 *"He who is wise <u>**wins**</u> souls"*

So, learning how to **actually, genuinely <u>win</u>** souls is what wisdom is all about.

It takes faithfulness *according to God's terminology of faithfulness;*

…it takes walking in, *and yielding* to, God's will,

…that means, *walking out the nature of God!*

…it means, *walking out the love of God!*

…it means, walking *in <u>genuine</u> love,*

…in <u>generosity</u> and <u>mercy</u>,

…in order to experience God's power *and true riches*

I am reminded of what Jesus said in Matthew:

Matthew 6:33

33 *"**Seek first** (above all else; exclusively) the righteousness of God and His Kingdom,*

…*and all these things shall be added unto you.*"

But let's finish up in Luke 16:12-15,

12 *"And if you have not been faithful in what is another man's who will give you what is your own?"*

Mutual respect goes a long way!

If you have not been faithful *in your generosity; in real love and giving mutual respect,*

…and you have just only been giving and blessing other people, **who will give back to you** houses, cars, vacations *or any other things you want,*

*…*and this also refers to those of you, who have given your life to the ministry,

*…*if you have just done for others, *because of what they can give back to you,* **you my friend have been doing everything you do from the wrong motivation,** and sooner or later you will sacrifice all kinds of relationships and throw people under the bus supposedly for the sake of your vision, but really, for the sake of your own self-centered greed,

*…*and then when those hidden agendas, and those secret motives of the heart rises to the surface, then *who will continue supporting you in ministry?*

13 *"No servant can serve two masters; for either he will hate the one, and love the other, or else he will be loyal to the one, and despise the other"*

"You cannot serve God and mammon."

14 *"Now the Pharisees,* **who were lovers of money**

(I take it as also saying that they *were experts in financial matters,* they were experts *in the wisdom of this world*),

"…they also heard all these things, and **they turned up their noses at Him***…"*

They snubbed Him; *they thought they knew better;*

…they refused to hear, **because they were in bondage to their own greed and legalism***;*

*…***to the wisdom of this world!**

That wisdom was speaking in their hearts and to their minds and saying:

'*He is a fool.*'

'*He doesn't know what He is talking about.*'

15 *"But He said to them:* '**You are those who <u>justify yourselves</u> before men***"*

(*…***you make excuses within yourself for the rottenness that exists there; you are full of excuses** …**and you use your legalism and so-called wisdom, and supposed financial integrity, *to justify yourself before others*)**,

*"...**but God knows your hearts**."*

*"**For what is <u>highly esteemed</u> among men <u>is an abomination</u> in the sight of God.**"*

So to sum it all up, **in this parable Jesus was not giving us license to sin,**

...**He was not giving us an excuse to live irresponsibly financially,**

...**He is not saying squander all your money away on a whim.**

...**and He is not saying go out of your way to waste money,**

...**He was not condoning impulsive, compulsive behavior!**

...**but He was emphasizing that *building relationships and winning people's hearts over through generosity and real love,* <u>is more important</u> than money and the stuff we buy with it and own.**

I want you to listen carefully to what is being said.

I know this is a so-called hard teaching and difficult to receive.

You can easily dismiss it as wrong teaching or misconstrue what is being said,

...but I am asking you to *carefully consider what is being said.*

You still have to be discerning in relationships.

You still have to be prudent and wise, *but with a Godly wisdom,*

...with a heart of true love and mercy and generosity

You still have to let the Spirit of God lead you.

In another parable Jesus emphasized **that money and schedules and things like that** *should not take president over walking in mercy, kindness and love towards others,*

...in fact *walking in LOVE is the REAL issue.*

Chapter 4

Accountability and responsibility redefined

Luke 10:25-37

25 *"And it happened that a certain expert in the law stood up and tried to show Jesus to be a phony and a fraud by saying, 'Teacher, what shall I do **to inherit eternal life?**'*

26 *"Jesus responded to him by asking, 'What is written in the law? What is your reading of it?'*

27 *"So the man answered and said: **'You shall love the Lord your God with all your heart, with all your soul, with all your strength and with all your mind,' and 'your neighbor as yourself.'***

28 *"So Jesus said to him: 'You have answered correctly; **do this** and you will **live,***

*(…or, **you will truly have life!**)'*

29 *"But now the man felt put on the spot, and his conscience bothered him, **so wanting to justify himself**, he said to Jesus, 'And who exactly is my neighbor?'*

30 *"It was then that Jesus decided to answer him with a short parable;* **so everyone could clearly understand, and so no one could have any argument left in them***."*

He said:

'A certain man went down from Jerusalem to Jericho, but was overcome by thieves. They stripped him of his clothes and wounded him badly. They took off and left him for dead."

31 *"Now by chance a certain priest came down the road…"*

He was probably a very busy man with a tight schedule to keep *places to go, and people to see*.

Perhaps he was already running a little late for the Wednesday night prayer gathering that he was supposed to lead,

…besides he was a respected man in society, what would people think of him hanging out on the side of the road with a low-life gentile?

'I mean the man doesn't even look like a Jew, and he obviously did something wrong to deserve such a beating. Maybe his sins finally caught up to him, and I would be interfering with God's punishment of him if I were to help him now, you know;

…It could also be a trap,

…wisdom would suggest that I not stop and put my own life at risk here.

…Getting involved is such a bother you know;

…besides I don't really want to waste God's money, or my valuable time helping some poor unfortunate schmuck.'

31 *"…and when he saw him, he passed by on the other side."*

32 *"Likewise a Levite, when he arrived at the scene, came over and looked,* (but after having the same conversation with himself as the priest did) *passed by on the other side."*

33 *"But a certain Samaritan…"*

(Not only did Jews not mix with gentiles in those days, but there was also racial segregation between Jews and Samaritans. In fact Samaritans were the mixed offspring of the Jews and the gentile people who also lived in the same territory.

They were considered outcasts themselves by the Jews and marginalized for their mixed heritage.)

33 *"But a certain Samaritan, as he journeyed…"*

(…indicating that he traveled a long way, *so he wasn't even from around there*)

*"...he came over to where the man was lying on the ground. And when he saw the man, **he had compassion on him**."*

Now this man probably also had places to go and people to see.

He probably was also on his way to an appointment.

Maybe he had his money all budgeted out for the journey and couldn't really afford to spend any on this man either.

I mean no one likes to waste money,

...especially on something you didn't plan for and that just kind of came upon you so suddenly; *just kind of fell in your lap to take care of.*

'Why didn't the priest stop to help this man, or the Levite for that matter, I mean it's their job isn't it, besides they live around here, I'm not even from this town. I'm not even related to this man; I mean the man looks like a Jew,' the Samaritan could have reasoned.

'Why should I waste my precious time and recourses to help this total stranger? Where is his family or friends anyway?'

33 *"...and when he saw the man, **he had compassion on him**."*

34 *"He went over to the man and bandaged his wounds, pouring on oil and wine; and he set him on his own animal,* **brought him to an inn, <u>and took care of him</u>***."*

35 *"On the next day, when he departed, he took out whatever amount of money was needed, gave it to the innkeeper, and then promised him that he would come by there again and repay him if he would only take care of the man until he was better."*

"He said: 'Take care of him; and whatever more you spend, when I come again, I will repay you.'

36 **'So,' Jesus said, 'which one of these three do you think was a real neighbor and friend to the man who got attacked by the thieves?'**

37 *"And reluctantly the man replied,* **'He who showed mercy on the wounded man,'**

"...but Jesus challenged him once again and said, '<u>**Go and do likewise**</u>*.'"*

Jesus emphasized that LOVE must rule supreme;

...and quite often loving people means *spending time, money and other resources.*

Love, generosity, liberality, kindness, hospitality, friendship and fellowship,

...these are all words that are almost synonymous, because they are inseparably linked.

I do think I have to caution you though.

Sometimes people look at these teachings of Scripture *and they feel **justified** in their sins,*

...they feel that they have found some kind of agreement with their way of thinking, *and now have a license to continue to show **a lack of integrity;***

...they feel all *liberated from **any kind of financial responsibility,***

...and as far as being people of their word *is concerned,*

*...but their warped, so-called liberty **is nothing other than just a spirit of rebellion against society,***

*...and it quickly puts them **right back into bondage.***

They end up being *a poor witness for Jesus*.

They think they found *an excuse* **to live irresponsible lives when it comes to finances and schedules and things,** *but they are deceived and mistaken*.

Bondage awaits that kind of stinking thinking also, just as much, if not more, *than legalism.*

Licentiousness *is worse than legalism.*

Paul says in Romans 6 that **God's truths are** *not an excuse to miss the mark.*

God wants us to be free <u>from anxiety</u>, *not integrity.*

He doesn't want us to be irresponsible, lazy or neglectful people *who live in licentiousness and cannot be trusted.*

God wants us living in His will; living by His nature and His character and His love that is our portion and that we are partakers of,

...He wants us living by our true design, by the image and likeness of God within our inner man,

...by that image and likeness we were designed for, *and in which we were in fact designed and made and brought forth,*

...these things are already deposited within us; we were born with it, in our spirit,

...God wants us living in His will; He wants us living in these things, expressing these things, *where there is true freedom,*

...He doesn't want us living off to the left, or off to the right of it!

So in this book I want us to consider *our real accountability,*

...and rethink the whole concept of responsibility *from God's perspective* in the Scriptures as we study the Word,

...*without becoming irresponsible, or licentious people, with no integrity*

Now let's get into the meat of what I really want to show you in this book.

I first of all want to bring to your attention that *God's commitment to you in covenant* is of such a nature,

...that *God has totally dedicated Himself to provide you with your daily needs.*

Chapter 5

Survival or abundance

Matthew 6:19-21, 25-34

19 *"Do not lay up for yourselves treasure on earth, where moth and rust consumes, and where thieves break in and steal,"*

20 *"...but lay up for yourselves treasure in heaven, where neither moth nor rust consumes, and where thieves do not break in and steal."*

21 *"For where your treasure is, there your heart will be also,"*

(...or, **what you treasure has your heart!**)

25 *"I tell you, do not be anxious about your life, what you shall eat, or what you shall drink, nor about your body, what you shall put on. Is not life more than food and the body more than clothing?"*

26 *"Look at the birds of the air, they neither sow, nor reap, nor gather into barns, and yet **your** Heavenly Father feeds them. **Are you not of more value to Him than they?"***

27 *"Can any of you through anxiety add a single hour to your span of life?"*

28 *"Why are you anxious about clothing? Consider the flowers of the fields; they neither toil nor spin"*

29 *"…yet I tell you, even Solomon in all his glory was not arrayed like one of these."*

30 *"If God so clothes the grass of the fields, which is alive today and dead tomorrow and can be thrown into the oven, **will He not much more clothe you, O you of little faith?"***

31 *"Therefore, do not be anxious saying: 'What shall we eat?' or 'What shall we drink?' or 'What shall we wear?'*

32 *"For the gentiles **seek** all these things; indeed **your** Heavenly Father **knows that you need all these things"***

33 *"But seek first* (as your highest priority; exclusively) *the righteousness of God and His Kingdom* (He is talking about your spirit identity) *and all these things shall be added unto you."*

34 *"Therefore do not be anxious about tomorrow…"*

Jesus says in verse 25 & 26

25 *"Do not be anxious,* **as your Heavenly Father feeds the birds, He will feed you also**.*"*

26 **"Truth is He is much more dedicated to feed you than the birds**, *o you of little faith."*

He says in verse 28 & 29

28 *"Why are you anxious about clothing?* **Consider the flowers of the fields**, *that they neither toil nor spin,"*

29 *"…yet I tell you, even Solomon in all his glory was not arrayed like one of these."*

Have you ever considered the flowers of the fields how they grow?

Have you considered the variety of color that they display, and fragrance that they diffuse?

They are your Father's idea and invention; they are a product of your Father's thought.

I am not in agreement with certain sects that believe we are only supposed to wear drab looking black, khaki or blue colored clothes, *because you don't just get khaki shrubs or blue flowers.*

God says:

28 *"consider the flowers; consider* **their color, their fragrance, their beauty**.*"*

29 *"Solomon, in all his glory, could not be arrayed as one of them"*

The same Father who arrayed them and clothed them in color, in fragrance and in beauty *is dedicated to clothe you with beauty, hallelujah, not with rags.* **Amen!**

God did not clothe any flower with rags, **and they don't even toil or spin.**

He says in verse 30,

30 *"If God so clothes the grass of the fields* **which is alive today and dead tomorrow** *and can be thrown into the oven…"*

I don't know about you but I'm going to have a better future than today or tomorrow,

Hallelujah!

Thank God we've got a bigger future than tomorrow friend, you better believe it!

In Christ Jesus you can have a covenant relationship and a better future than today or tomorrow,

…a glorious eternal future in Him and in Heaven, amen!

Unless you're like the man who was building larger barns, *who lost his whole future that night when he died anyway,*

68

...regardless of the size of his barns!

Luke 12:15-21

15 *"And then He said to them (the whole crowd), **'Take heed and <u>beware of covetousness, for one's life does not consist in the abundance of the things he possesses.'</u>***

16 *"Then He spoke a parable to them, saying: 'The ground of a certain rich man yielded plentifully."*

17 *"And he thought within himself, saying, 'What shall I do, since I have no more room to store my crops?'*

18 *"So he said, 'I will do this: I will pull down my barns and build greater, and there I will store all my crops and my goods."*

19 *"And I will say to my soul, 'Soul, you have many goods laid up for many years; take your ease; eat, drink, and be merry.'*

(He sounds to me like a self-made man, a man of wisdom according to the systems of this world)

20 *"**But God said to him, 'You fool!'***

*'This night your soul will be required of you **then whose will those things be which you have provided?'***

21 '*So is he who lay up treasure for himself,
and is not rich toward God.*'

But let's return to Matthew 6:30

30 *"If God so clothes the grass of the fields,
which is alive today and dead tomorrow and
can be thrown into the oven, **will He not much
more clothe you, O you of little faith**?"*

You see that **the measure of *our faith* has
something to do with the provision we
enjoy.**

Jesus refers here to *"little faith."*

Do you see that it's possible **to have little
faith?**

…or, to have ***almost no faith?***

…or, ***small faith?***

And if it's possible to have *little faith,*

…*then it's also possible to have **a larger
measure,***

…*a larger faith,*

…***strong faith!***

But what I'm saying is that **the measure** of our
faith, not faith **for** something, but **the measure
of His faith**; the measure of **our faith in Him,**

...**that measure, living in us;** *alive within us,* *has everything to do with our daily practical experience of provision.*

Often we have missed it in our faith teaching, in seeing faith as *believing* **for** *something;*

...*as believing* **to get** *something,*

...while **true Bible faith,** *true New Testament faith,* **is not something you can still get,**

...**it is something** <u>you already have</u> **in God's covenant commitment to you.**

That *measure* **is available to you** *in His Word*;

...**it's available in** *what He has already said to you and revealed about Himself concerning you in His Word; in Christ Jesus,*

...*which the Scriptures bear strong witness to!*

How do <u>*you*</u> **measure that commitment; that dedication, that devotion, that love?**

<u>**Do you measure it accurately**</u>**?**

Is it The Truth of God?

...**or is it the merely the words of men?**

It makes all the difference in the world.

It will affect your faith I guarantee it.

I want you to really hear what I am saying.

It is such a different concept about faith.

It makes such a big difference **to know** what you *have* in **Him**;

…it is so different *to discover* **what you already** *have*,

…than to have to try and work it out in your faith,

…and to having to put your faith out for the next project,

…putting your faith out for your toothpaste,

…putting your faith out for your next pair of shoes,

…putting your faith out for a meal!

We have developed this terminology in error *and it has set our eyes on our own efforts and our own ability,*

…and our own faith,

…and it has taken us straight back into works, fear, and self-doubt!

No wonder we struggle with faith,
wondering if we will ever have enough faith.

Listen, love is the fuel of faith.

Love Himself is the fuel of our faith.

The power of faith is rooted *in God's initiative,*

*…***in His provision,**

*…***in His person,**

*…***in His love for you,**

*…***in His character,**

*…***in His covenant commitment towards you**

And so, we want to discover the basis of *Bible faith, of New Testament faith,*

*…because that faith releases us to be free from **any** financial **concern**, from **any financial anxiety and stress**, from **any** material **anxiety and greed related to it**.*

God wants us to be free from anxiety, amen!

And if there has been one area in particular that has snared minister after minister, and ministry after ministry, *it's been this area of finances **because of anxiety**.*

All you have to do is read some of the newsletters you receive in the mail every day to see it.

Matthew 6:30

30 *"If God so clothes the grass of the fields, which is alive today and dead tomorrow and can be thrown into the oven, **will He not much more** clothe you, O you of little faith?"*

Every time I read the words: *"**MUCH MORE**"* in the Scriptures, I get my thickest highlighter or my thickest pen out and I highlight it, **because that's God's measure,**

...and I want to continue to fuel my faith with God's measure.

He came to give us life **more abundantly,** amen!

Listen, God is not committed to your survival; *He's committed to your success!*

The world system; anxiety, fear, greed, legalism has only one theme and it is called *survival!*

...but God wants you to enjoy *the much-more-ness* of His provision.

*"...will He not **much more** clothe you, **O you of little faith?**"* — Matthew 6:30

74

Chapter 6

Make-believe wealth versus real treasure

Matthew 6:30 & 31

30 *"...will He not **much more** clothe you, **O you of little faith?**"*

31 *"Therefore do not be anxious **saying**: 'What shall we eat?' or 'What shall we drink?' or 'What shall we wear?'*

It's interesting to see that Jesus refers here *to our confession,*

...to our language that gives expression to our anxiety!

Did you know that your anxiety *speaks?*

Your anxiety is not something *you can hide in your heart.*

Become anxious enough and you'll soon find yourself *talking your anxiety.*

Now did you know that faith works the same way?

If you really believe you'll soon *talk your faith.*

Anxiety is always *problem conscious.*

Faith is always *provision conscious.*

In 2Corinthians 4:13 Paul writes and he says:

13 *"We have the same spirit of faith, as he had who wrote. He said: '**I believe and so I speak**.' So we too believe and so we speak."*

There's another little Scripture, in Matthew 16, I want us to take note of,

...now remember Jesus said:

*"...do not be anxious for your life **saying:** 'What shall we eat?"*

But here in Matthew 16 *the disciples are with Jesus in His very presence,*

...I mean they are daily seeing the manifestations of His glorious provision, of His power, and of the miracles, and it was wonderful,

...**but they've become so dominated through their years of education by natural things** that,

...here they are in the boat, *with Jesus, in His very presence,* discussing the fact that they have not brought any bread with them.

Matthew 16:7 & 8

7 *"And they reasoned among themselves, saying, 'It is because we have taken no bread.'*

8 *"But Jesus aware of this said: "O men of little faith.* **Why do you discuss among yourselves <u>the fact</u>** *that you have no bread?"*

Listen, discussing <u>the facts</u> destroys faith!

I mean, just keep at it, just keep discussing the facts, *and you'll soon discover that I'm right in what I'm saying.*

Your faith will be destroyed.

Sometimes we think it's a very responsible thing to do, you know, we're going to have a board meeting now, you know, *and we're going to just discuss the financial problems of our household, or of our ministry.*

I guarantee that the longer you discuss <u>the facts</u>, *the sooner you destroy your faith.*

Anxiety always wants to dominate you, *through your confession.*

Matthew 16:9 -11 Jesus says:

9 *"**<u>Do you not yet perceive</u>, do you not recall** the five loaves, or the five thousand, and how many baskets you gathered?"*

10 *"Or the seven loaves, and the four thousand, and how many baskets you gathered?"*

11 ***"How is it that you fail to perceive?"***

(And then he got back to the real topic He was talking about earlier)

"I wasn't even referring to bread!

…I was warning you to beware of the leaven, **the influence** *of the Pharisees and Sadducees; I was speaking* **about the influence of their teachings,** *not bread."*

11 ***"How is it that you fail to perceive?"***

The Spirit of God desires to release our minds from anxiety that would limit our lives to temporal values.

And I am telling you now; the only way He can do this, the only way He can set our minds free,

…is _when we discover the worth of our lives_, beyond natural value, beyond price.

Matthew 6:26

26 *"Look at the birds of the air, they neither sow, nor reap, nor gather into barns, and* **yet, _your_ Heavenly Father feeds them**.*"*

"Are you not of more value to Him than they?"

Matthew 6:31 & 32

31 "**Therefore, do not be anxious, saying**: *'What shall we eat?' or 'What shall we drink?' or 'What shall we wear?'*

32 *"For **the gentiles seek all these things**…"*

Jesus is not referring to the gentiles *in a prejudice way.*

He is not referring to them in a way to try and belittle them, *but in terms of the fact that at that portion of time the gentiles did not have a covenant with God that anyone was aware of, although they already did as far as God was concerned, but I am not getting into all of that right now,*

…you will have to go read my book on "God's Eternal Purpose!" if you want an understanding into that subject,

Ha… ha… ha…

How is that for the use of worldly wisdom and marketing strategies of promotion! ☺

He is speaking to Jews here remember, so He refers to the gentiles in terms of *those who are outside of the promises, outside of the covenant with God that the Jews had.*

Remember when Jesus, on the Sabbath, released that woman who was bent over for 18 years?

Do you remember Him referring to her as being, *"...a daughter of Abraham whom Satan has bound these 18 years?"*

Jesus was implying that she was *a daughter of covenant,*

...and therefore need not have suffered for all those years.

Her ignorance kept her in bondage to Satan in her mind and in her thinking and in her spirit, to the accuser of the brethren, *to that legalistic voice of accusation and condemnation that tells you and assures you that you never measure up!*

Her ignorance, her embrace of that voice of accusation, kept her in bondage to that debilitating disease then as well!

...because, *ultimately it all comes from Satan!*

Her ignorance kept her in bondage to Satan in her mind and in her thinking and in her spirit, and therefore also to sickness and disease in her body!

Now here in this Scripture (Matthew 6:32) **Jesus was reminding them that they as Jews had *a covenant with God*,**

...so they should have faith and should not have to live their lives the way the gentiles had to, who had no prominent covenant in their history to be able to refer back to.

Through faith, the Jews could have lived their lives differently from the gentiles.

The gentiles, *those who were outside of covenant knowledge;* they had to survive on this planet.

So they had to pursue these things:

They had to rely on their own wisdom and they had to rely on themselves, on their own worldly wisdom, the wisdom of gathering together into barns, sowing and reaping and spinning and toiling...

(I want you to hear me well.

I don't want people to misquote me from this teaching and say that I said that believers are supposed to ignore wisdom altogether, and that believers aren't supposed to have jobs, that believers aren't supposed to work, that believers aren't supposed to gather together and sow and reap etc.

I want you to hear accurately the principle of what we are looking at in the Scriptures.

We are looking at covenant knowledge and how it relates to anxiety,

…and how it relates to provision!

…we are talking about our true value and worth,

…the way God sees us, as His own dear children,

…and how it relates to anxiety,

…as well as provision,

…we are not talking about living irresponsible lives and thinking we have a license to sin.)

Matthew 6:31 & 32

31 *"Therefore **do not be anxious saying**: 'What shall we eat?' or 'What shall we drink?' or 'What shall we wear?'*

32 *"For the gentiles seek all these things,*

*…**but listen, your Heavenly Father knows that you need them all**."*

33 *"**<u>BUT seek first</u>** (as your highest pursuit, exclusively) **His righteousness and His Kingdom** (your true spirit identity)…"*

He doesn't say:

'Don't seek these things'

He says:

"**BUST seek first** (as your highest pursuit, exclusively) *His righteousness and His Kingdom* (your true spirit identity)…"

His Kingdom speaks of *His dominion, the dominion of His truth and of His love in and through your personal life,*

…and righteousness is *the platform upon which that dominion is established;*

That righteousness; that platform of faith and confidence within **you which establishes His dominion within you and through you,** *is in fact, your true spirit identity you have from God,* **who you really are,**

*…***because you are His image and likeness,**

*…***because you are His child,**

*…***you come from above.**

"Righteousness establishes Your throne," says David.

The righteousness of faith, believing these realities I just mentioned …*it is fully embracing these things that release His* *dominion, His reign, in your life.*

Then what does He say?

'You'll never get hungry again so there is no need for food, and you'll never need to wear clothes again, because the need for it will disappear.'

NO!

Matthew 6:33

He says:

33 *"...**ALL THESE OTHER THINGS SHALL BE ADDED UNTO YOU AS WELL**."*

34 *"**Therefore, do not be anxious** about tomorrow..."*

Did you hear that?

*"**ALL THESE THINGS SHALL BE ADDED UNTO YOU!!!**"*

Do you believe it?

1Peter 5:7

7 *"**Cast all your anxieties upon Him <u>for it matters to Him about you, in fact, He cares for you</u>**."*

Matthew 6:19-21

19 *"Do not lay up for yourselves treasure on earth, where moth and rust consumes, and where thieves break in and steal,"*

20 *"but, lay up for yourselves, treasure in heaven* (in the unseen realm of spirit reality), *where neither moth nor rust consumes, and where thieves do not break in and steal."*

21 *"<u>For where your treasure is, there your heart will be also</u>"*

I believe that God has rustproof living in mind for us,

...**RUSTPROOF LIVING**.

Hallelujah!

I believe God wants us to treasure *that which is eternal*,

...**His steadfast love for us,**

...**and His eternal, unshakable Word;**

...**His truth revealed concerning us,**

...**who we are to Him,**

...**our true spirit identity,**

...**and our value to Him,**

...because of who He says we are.

When we begin to discover our wealth in God, *in who He is towards us, and who we are to Him,* we discover that we have a wealth beyond decay.

You see if we limit our wealth to natural value, *we deceive ourselves.*

Chapter 7

The greater measure

The whole way the world system thinks is wrong.

The world system has valued people *in terms of their talent, in terms of their experience, in terms of their education.*

The world system has valued people *in only one measure, the measure of finances,*

…in other words, *what you are worth an hour, or what you are worth a month in terms of salary.*

I dare say that the whole salary system of this world *is built on deception.*

I don't believe that God had a salary system in mind for man originally.

I don't think He ever had that in mind for us!

I know I am saying bold things, and there is no way I could feel free enough to say it, *unless God has revealed to us some alternative,* **which He has!**

What God has revealed is better than a salary, **to measure our worth by, and to live by.**

I say again:

God, in Christ Jesus, has already in all reality given us an alternative that is better than salary, *to measure our worth by and to live by!*

Remember how God educated His people under the old Jewish Covenant *to bring of the first fruits to the storehouse that there may be food in God's house.*

God introduced them to the whole tithing principle.

But we need to understand that this principle was introduced **during a time of broken relationship**

It was introduced to fallen man *in his fallen state, as a fallen creature with a fallen mindset!*

It was introduced *to educate him <u>to go beyond</u> his fears and his natural mindset and its tendencies*

The mindset of fallen man is *to gather,*

…and to hold for himself,

…for the sake of survival, lest he perish!

88

The mindset and therefore the tendency of fallen man *is to be selfish,*

*…*and even within his own household, within his own family, among his own loved ones,

…it is hard for him to go beyond that mindset, **and break free from his fallen thinking, as being merely a natural creature.**

Galatians chapter 3 speaks of how God had to educate fallen man *through the Law.*

The Law dealt with fallen man *like a schoolteacher would educate a child.*

Galatians 3:23

23 *"Now* **before faith came,**

…we were confined under the Law,

…kept in constraint,

*…***until faith should be revealed**.*"*

24 *"So that the Law was our teacher,*

*…***until Christ came***

(…and why did He come)*

*…***that we** *(in other words, since he came we)* **might be justified by faith**.*"*

25 *"But <u>after faith has come,</u>*

...we are no longer under a custodian."

Another translation says:

25 *"<u>BUT NOW THAT FAITH HAS COME,</u>*

...WE NO LONGER NEED A CUSTODIAN."

(I do believe that this Scripture directly applies to tithing as well.)

Do not get confused now and think that I am speaking out against giving *and so affording people an excuse not to give generously to the ongoing work of God by the Church.*

I am not coming against giving or against tithing.

I do want you to understand, however, that tithing *is just a limited measure,*

...and that **we are now under a new system,**

...a new law, the law of Christ,

...the law of His love,

...<u>the government of faith!</u>

"Faith works BY LOVE" - Galatians 5:6

His love and truth inspires our faith!

90

Faith comes into our lives _to release us_ into an even greater measure.

The principle of tithing God taught the Israelites was a very good custodian _for fallen Man._

That custodian was there to _make sure that Israel keeps on giving_ **at a certain minimum measure at least**.

Its purpose was to release fallen Man _into a measure of blessing,_

…to help him _go beyond his natural fear-based mindset,_

…to help him _to break free, at least to some degree, from his fallen thinking,_

…**to at least reach a certain measure of generosity, and experience its blessing!**

But now we also know that **it fell short and could not achieve even this minimum measure of success,**

…otherwise Malachi 3:7-12 would never have needed to be written.

Malachi 3:7-12

7 **"Yet, from the days of your fathers, you have gone away from my ordinances, and have not kept them.**

'Return to Me, and I will return to you,' says the Lord of hosts.

But you said: 'In what way shall we return?'

8 *'Will a man rob God?'*

Yet, you have robbed Me!

But you say, 'In what way have we robbed You?'

…In tithes and offerings"

9 **"You are cursed with a curse,**

(Listen, He was not talking about Him cursing them, NO, *He was speaking about the government of sin that ruled over fallen Man*),

"You are cursed with a curse, even this whole nation;

…I can see it clearly in your robbing of Me!"

He then felt the need to enforce the principle of tithing yet once again,

…but really he was writing prophetically *about the coming of Christ!*

He would be God's own tithe *that satisfies God.*

He would be the fulfillment,

*…***of every prophetic picture in the Old Covenant *hidden in the Law, and spoken about by the prophets!***

10 *"Bring the whole tithe into the storehouse that there may be food in my house.* (This was a prophetic reference to the coming of Jesus. The fullness was revealed in Him. He is the whole tithe! The fullness of the release comes through Him!)

*…***And prove Me now in this,' says the Lord of Hosts,**

(Write it down, and test Me on this; you can prove Me on this, you can take it to the bank and it will spend!

*…look to see if what I am about to say will come to pass, **for it surely will, in the Messiah, in Christ!***)

Bank on it, you can bet your life on it, look to see,

'If I will not open for you the windows of heaven and pour out for you such blessing that there will not be room enough to receive it.'

11 *"**And I will rebuke the devourer for your sakes,***

...*so that he will not (be able to) destroy the fruit of your ground (anymore),*

...*nor shall the vine fail to bear fruit for you in the field,'* *says the Lord of hosts;"*

12 *'**And all nations shall call you blessed, for you will be a delightful land,**' says the Lord of hosts."*

This effort to keep the Law from falling short and to get fallen Man to at least attain to a certain measure of giving and blessing went on ***until Christ came and introduced a new and better way, a new and better system than the Law***.

The Law and it's principle of tithing fell short, *because of the weakness of fallen Man (**being ruled by the government of sin**,)* according to Romans 8:2-4,

...it fell short, **and was therefore done away with in Christ.**

Romans 8:1-4

1 *"There is therefore now no condemnation for those who are in Christ Jesus"*

2 *"For the law of the Spirit of life in Christ Jesus **has made me free** from the law of sin and death"*

3 *"For what the Law could not do in that **it was weak through the flesh**"*

(Note: The government of sin manipulates and controls Man's flesh *through Man's fallen thinking,*

...through that stronghold of deception established since the fall in the mind of Man,

...from there; from that thinking, from that fallen mindset, from that stronghold of deception in Man's mind, in Man's thinking, it operated and ruled Man),

So *"...what the Law could not do ...**God did***

...by sending His own Son in the likeness of sinful flesh,

...to come and deal with sin!

...As far is sin is concerned: **He condemned (and killed) *sin in the flesh!***

(He destroyed its power; He broke its stronghold; He removed its legal right to rule ...its assumed right ...assumed through lies and deception,

...He (Jesus) destroyed that so called right),

4 *"...**so that the righteous requirements of the law might be fulfilled <u>in us</u>***

*…**those of us, who,** do not **walk** according to the flesh, but **according to the Spirit,***

*…**according to our restored spirit identity***"

Romans 8:1

1 *"There is therefore **NOW**…"*

What does he mean *"**NOW?**"*

Since when or what?

I mean what happened that brought about the *"NOW"* he is referring to?

He is talking about: **since faith came,**

*"**NOW that faith has come,**"*

*"**NOW**"* that we are *"**in Christ Jesus,**"* under a new system.

1 *"There is therefore **NOW** no condemnation **for those who are in Christ Jesus**…"*

How can he say *"no condemnation?"*

How can we achieve *"NO CONDEMNATION?"*

2 *"For* (or we can, because) **the law of the Spirit of life** in Christ Jesus **has made me free** from the law of sin and death."*

Because we are in Christ,

96

...this powerful Spirit of life that is in Christ,

...this powerful new law of the Spirit,

...this powerful new government of the Spirit,

...this powerful new system that produces life has come into operation in our lives.

This new system He is talking about *is the principle of faith* we live our lives by,

...it is that faith that came in Jesus Christ!

That same faith of God, that linked us to the life of Christ, has also set us free from the government, from the law of sin and death.

That principle of faith, that spirit of faith, that powerful Spirit of life in Christ, has set us free from, and elevated us above, sin's power, and death's power.

Hallelujah!

3 *"For what the Law* (the system, or the principles under the old covenant, **tithing included**) *could not do in that it was weak through the flesh* (or through sin which ruled over the flesh, from that stronghold in Man's thinking)*,"*

"...For what the Law (and every principle under that old covenant and that old system) *could*

*not do **GOD DID** by sending His own Son* in *the likeness of sinful flesh,* **to come and deal with sin.** *As far is sin is concerned: He condemned* (and killed) *sin in the flesh,"*

(That means: **He rendered it powerless and defeated it; He broke its power over the flesh;**

...He stripped it of its legal right to rule ...its assumed right ...assumed through lies and deception,

...and thus He broke its power over the flesh,

...because He challenged the lie and deception,

...and defeated it,

...and broke it,

...and rendered it powerless!)

4 *"so that the righteous requirements of the law* (...the law of Christ now, the law of the new creation, not the Law of Moses now, but that perfect law of liberty, that law of Christ that perfectly liberates us, might be fulfilled in us who believe.)

...He is talking about that which the Law and its principles tried to achieve in us) *might actually NOW be fulfilled in us and by us,*

who do not **walk** according to the flesh, but **according to the Spirit**."

The old system and its principles are done away with.

It is no longer employed in the New Testament as a principle and a means by which to live to please the Father.

A new system with a new principle, the principle of faith alone, the very faith of God is employed,

...that truth and faith that came in Jesus Christ,

...that truth and faith by which we now live to express the will of the Father!

We now live under a new system; a new principle in Christ, the principle of a changed life, which has now become our experience, through embracing the truth and faith revealed in Him.

It is by very definition more powerful than the principle of tithing, *or any other principle under the old system.*

Let's also read Colossians 2:11-23

11 *"In Him you were also circumcised with the circumcision made without hands,*

...the body of the sins of the flesh (the government of sin ruling over the flesh) was put off by the circumcision of Christ"

12 *"as you were immersed into Him...*

("By one Spirit we were immersed into one body,

...and have all been made to drink into one Spirit." 1Corinthians 12:13)

"...as you were immersed into Him, you were not only buried with Him, **but you were also raised** *with Him* **into newness of life** *through God's faith;*

...through that faith in God's working when He raised Him from the dead..."

(Romans 4:25 says that *"He was delivered up* **because of** *our offences, and was raised* **because of** *our justification")*

13 **"So you who were dead in your trespasses and the un-circumcision of your flesh (the government of sin ruling over your flesh), He has made alive in Him, having forgiven you all trespasses**,"

14 *"...***because He had wiped out the certificate of debt that was against us, condemning us**"

"He took it out of the way *by nailing it to the cross."*

15 **"In doing this He disarmed principalities and powers** *and made a public spectacle of them; He triumphed over them in this."*

16 **"Therefore, let no one judge you any longer** *in what you can eat and what you can drink,*

...or as far as whether you observe festivals or a new moon or even Sabbaths for that matter,

(...*or whatever principle or ritual, that was a part of that old religious system, even tithing),"*

17 *"...***which were only supposed to be mere shadows of <u>the things</u> to come anyway,**

*...***but now <u>those things</u> are here,**

*...***the substance is of Christ.***"*

18 *"***Let no one defraud you of your freedom or your reward**

(...*let no one put you back in bondage in other words),*

...he is talking about those taking delight in false humility and even the worship of angels,

...intruding into (or violating) **those things they have very little understanding of,**

*…he says, "…they are **vainly puffed up in their fleshly, old system, religious mindset**,"*

19 *"…**and not holding fast to Christ the head,***

*…from whom all the body, **nourished and knitted together** by joints and ligaments (**by the new covenant truths of the Word**), grows* (and matures and bears fruit) *with the increase* (of understanding and faith) *which comes from God"*

20 *"Therefore, if you died with Christ **from the basic principles this world lives by,***

*…**any kind of old religious system, or flesh ruled system,***

*…why then, **as though you are still of this world**, living in the wisdom of this world,*

*…**why do you subject yourselves to its ignorance?***

*…I am talking about **its foolish legalism,***

*…**its old system of religious regulations** that say:"*

21 *'Do not touch, do not taste, do not handle,'*

22 *"…which all concern things which perish with the using of it …**these things are all just the commandments and doctrines of men**,"*

23 *"...**Self-imposed religion,***

*...**false humility,***

*...**and the neglect of one's body,***

*...these things indeed **has an appearance of wisdom**,*

*...but **are of no value** against the indulgence of the flesh,*

(...really, they cannot curb the indulgence of the government of sin ruling over the flesh)"

(Only the truth revealed in Christ Jesus can set a person free *and keep them free!*)

3:1 *"**Seeing then that you were raised with Christ <u>to newness of life</u>**...*"

(In other words, sin's power over you has been broken.

"Our old man was crucified with Him, so that (meaning that) *the body of sin* [the government of sin ruling in our lives] *might* (now) *be done away with; **we should no longer be slaves of sin*** (we don't have to be anymore)*"*
- Romans 6:6.

You can go ahead and read the whole of Romans chapter 6 for that matter)

Colossians 3:1

3:1 "**_Seeing then_ that you were raised with Christ _to newness of life_,**"

2 "*Set your mind on things above, not on things on the earth.*"

(Ephesians 2:6 says,

6 "*...seek those things, which are above, where Christ **and you** are seated right now at the right hand of God the Father.*")

Colossians 3:3

3 "**For you died,** and **your life is hidden with Christ in God**."

4 "*Whenever Christ, **who is our life,** appears, you also will appear with Him, **as having the same glory**"*

In the light of this, let's now get back to talking about *the principles of the Law under the old covenant,*

...and especially the principle of tithing

The principle of tithing was a good principle, *it wasn't a bad principle,* **but there was a problem with it**.

There was a problem with the old system.

It tried to bring in a greater measure of life,

…**but instead it brought a greater measure of condemnation**.

It had a reverse effect, *not because it in and of itself was wrong, but **it fell short**.*

It didn't have the power to change people.

It only served to provoke sin, ruling over the mentality and flesh of fallen Man,

…**and therefore produced greater rebellion and death** *instead of greater more abundant life and liberty*.

You can go read all of Romans chapter 7 and 2 Corinthians chapter 3 if you want a better understanding of this.

There are also many other places in the New Testament where this topic is discussed, like in the book of Galatians for instance.

It is very vitally important that you get a thorough grasp on these things.

I have also written about this in more detail in several other books I have written, like *"No Longer Looking for Applause!"* and *"God's Revealed Plan for Man,"* and *"God's Measure versus Man's Measure,"* as well as the one on *"Resurrection Life Now!"* and *"Reigning in Righteousness."* You are welcome to get them and read them. You will be enriched and enlightened some more; I guarantee it!

It is only the gospel of truth revealed in Jesus Christ that has the power to change people,

…the Law does not have enough eternal truth revealed in it to be able to do that,

…it is merely *a shadow* of that which was to come in Christ, *not the substance.*

"…the substance is of Christ!"
– Colossians 2:17

Chapter 8

Don't live a shortsighted life

The measure of success the Law tried to introduce *was just a mere shadow* **of the good things that came about in Christ.**

Christ in us, (revealed in us and indwelling us), is our hope of glory.

In Christ we are empowered to live beyond the limited levels of success the custodian tried to maintain in the lives of the people of Israel.

God wants us to discover and treasure the fact that we are now partakers of the Divine nature *through the knowledge of Jesus, through the knowledge of eternal truth, through the knowledge of faith,*

...through the birth of that faith in us

God wants us to discover and treasure our nature *in terms of the new creation that came about in Christ*.

That is our true nature, *our original nature restored, our only nature*.

That nature is a nature of love.

It's a nature of preferring others,

...preferring one another,

...preferring the brethren above ourselves!

That nature is the nature of giving.

Listen to me carefully now:

YOU DONT HAVE A DUAL NATURE.

You don't have a new creation mentality and expression; a new nature, *and an old sinful nature.*

If you have two natures, *then part of you will have to go to Heaven, and the other part of you will have to go to hell,*

He... he... he...

Listen, *the old sinful nature,*

(The old government of sin *that operated from your old fallen mindset; from that deception that ruled your mind and your thinking,* and manipulated and controlled your flesh; that ruled you and influenced your conduct)

...that old mindset and deception is done away with in Christ

If you are in Christ, and you are, that is if you can only see it and embrace it and believe it, *then you are a new creation; you have a new nature, a new mentality and a new expression;*

...it's your one and only nature, your true nature, the original nature you were designed in.

Jesus came exclusively to reveal and restore us back to that original design;

...to release us to again give expression to our true design!

You were designed in the image and likeness of God, after the very nature of God,

...and in Christ you are restored in that nature.

Until we discover and treasure the nature of the new creation <u>as our own nature</u>;

...until we discover the nature of the new creation, the nature of love, as our nature to give;

...until we discover our new creation love nature as the basis of giving,

...our giving will always be reluctant;

...it will always have to be under compulsion,

…it will always have to be motivated by the Law,

…or by someone's need,

…working through guilt on our conscience, *to at least have some sympathy for them!*

But when we discover and treasure our true nature, *our one and only nature, the love nature of the new creation* (2Corinthians 5:17),

…then we discover a liberty,

…a deliverance from anything within us, *that could possibly cause us to withhold from blessing.*

Praise God!!!

I am totally convinced in my heart that, *because it's in the love nature of the new creation to give,*

…*it is God's purpose for us to live beyond stinginess and beyond lack.*

Jesus said:

"Are not two sparrows sold for a penny?"

We place very little value on pesky little common birds like sparrows; they are rather insignificant to us, they are of little worth to us,

I mean, just look at how many of them there are flying around out there. They are of little concern to us. Who cares about what happens to one little old sparrow?

...here today and gone tomorrow,

"Are not two sparrows sold for a penny? **And yet, not one of them falls to the ground without your Father noticing.**

Nothing escapes Him.

He takes note of it, because He really does care!

And if He cares that much about one little bird, then how much more does He not also care about you!

Therefore do not fear I tell you; <u>you are of more value</u>,

...you are not insignificant,

...you are worth much more than many sparrows!

It matters to Him about you;

...it matters to Him what happens to you,

...even the very hairs on your head are all numbered.*"*

This is truth, *God's truth!*

...it <u>is</u> the truth, amen!

And yet, how we have sold ourselves *for Man's evaluation of us!*

How we have sold ourselves *for a salary*.

Remember Judas **how he sold and lost himself**,

...how he betrayed Jesus *for 30 pieces of silver (a month's salary)*.

Now remember the women who broke the alabaster box, *who refused to count the cost*.

I know there's a lot of teaching on *counting the cost* going around in the body of Christ today.

It has escalated to the point *where we have counted a lot of things not worth doing for Jesus*,

...to the point where we have actually sold and lost ourselves *like Judas did,*

...*and that for mere money!*

We have betrayed *our birthright,*

...*by becoming cost conscious!*

We count the cost, and we count the cost, and we count the cost,

...until we have counted ourselves right out of doing something for God,

...until we have counted ourselves right into compromise,

...until we have counted ourselves right out of sacrificing anything for the Kingdom.

Hey listen, when you're <u>in love</u> with someone, <u>you don't count the cost</u>,

...not in terms of time, or in terms of effort,

...not even in terms of money!

When you were in love you probably spent hours on the phone, and lots of money to boot, *just like I did.*

Many guys out there travel long distances from where they go to school, **even if they have to hitch-hike,** *just to see their girlfriends!*

They burn the proverbial candle at both ends, *but do not even consider it as a burden on them, or a sacrifice.*

We never *count the cost* of even one of those gifts we lavish upon our loved ones.

It's just money after all!

We never thought:

'Well I'm a young man now, and I'm growing up now, and I'm beginning to date this girl, and if I want to marry this girl I'm really going to have to sit down first and count the cost first,

...for in case it might be too costly you know.'

If we had to sit down *and count the cost*, many of us probably never would have gotten married, *nor have <u>any</u> children*.

If you still *consider the cost*,

...*then you can be bought for the right price!*

...*or you can be talked into quitting*,

...and I guarantee you, *you will fail in ministry!*

Satan will make sure of it!

The devil will use *counting the cost* <u>to get you to feel cheated</u>;

...he will quickly get you <u>so very bitter</u> *you will leave the ministry altogether*.

Listen to me now, in ministry <u>*you cannot afford*</u> *to become cost minded*,

*...and **you cannot afford** <u>to become salary minded either</u>.*

If you still teach *counting the cost,*

...if you still teach, 'Work out your earning potential brother, figure out how much you want to earn and set your goal in ministry accordingly,'

...then you are teaching law that will soon become a restricting, choking force,

...cultivating greed and impure motives,

...cultivating ungodliness,

...which only leads to destruction!

...you will be pierced through with many sorrows *and finally quit and go find something else to do*, *I guarantee it ...because it won't be worth it brother.*

While you are still using that measure, it won't be worth it!

...and you see, not only are you under law and miserable,

...and defiled in your heart and in your spirit,

...but worse yet, *you are placing others under law,* ***and subjecting them to the same miserable impure defilement,***

…and as long as the law is still being considered, *as long as it is still being applied to your life, and to their lives,* the Scriptures makes it clear:

*"…as long as the Law is read **a veil remains.**"*

Another Scripture says

*"Those who live by the law **are under a curse.**"*

You and they will remain shortsighted, brother, *even unto blindness,*

…unable to understand what it means, or even to function as a new creation,

…unable to even properly function in the things of the Kingdom!

I am telling you now, that mindset, that religious thinking, that law, *that fleshly measure* will limit you *to the point of bondage,*

…*to the point of bearing almost no fruit!*

Hey, please listen now, *there's no cost to count before committing yourself to Jesus.*

You just fall in love with Him and His righteousness and His Kingdom and, man, you're in it, your committed, boots and all! Forget the cost! Amen!

116

Whatever is not of faith and love misses the mark!

It's sin, amen!

It falls short!

I remember when I first fell in love with Jesus.

Sacrifice was not in my vocabulary.

I never considered anything that was a sacrifice as being a sacrifice, *in terms of time, in terms of effort, in terms of money, in terms of what it would cost me,*

...and I still feel that way today.

...because I am still in love with Him, amen!

...and nothing else can take it away from me,

...it is the fire that burns within me,

...the passion, the zeal, the energy,

...He is my everything, amen!

I never considered anything that was a sacrifice as being a sacrifice, and I still don't!

I never considered anything in terms of what it would cost me!

That woman with the alabaster box,

…I mean, this poor woman you know, *she didn't sit there and say to herself:*

'I wonder if I should break this alabaster box. Boy oh boy… you know; **I worked the whole of last year for it***. Oh… no… it's terrible, I just can't do it. I just can't get myself to waste it. I tell you what I'll do, I'll just open its lid, you know, and just give Jesus a few little sprays from the bottle. I'll just sprinkle Jesus with a little bit of the fragrance, and I'll close it up again. And maybe next week I can do it again, you know, and that way I can just keep a little in reserve because you never know what tomorrow holds.'*

No!

She sat there **and in her spirit something began to whelm up** and she began to think:

'What is the most costly thing I have to give? What do I have that I can use as a vehicle to communicate the intensity of my love for Him?'

And suddenly that alabaster box came to mind.

And she was so overjoyed that she at least had that alabaster box, *because she desired to communicate her love!*

Love must be communicated.

She went and fetched that alabaster box **and she broke it and she ministered to Jesus,**

…and the Spirit of God began to prophesy through that ointment, the death, the burial and the resurrection of Jesus

You see, *God always interprets unselfish giving in terms of spirit value!*

…while man interprets that kind of heart in terms of foolishness, God interprets it as wisdom,

…as valuable and worth rewarding!

'What do you mean wasting your life at discipleship school?'

'What do you mean wasting your life in ministry?'

*'**Count the cost man!'***

*'**You are wasting your life!'***

*'**You could become a wonderful engineer or a wonderful businessperson for Jesus!'***

Maybe some of you young people might still become that,

…but you know how the world reasons:

'Why this waist?'

Why not sell the alabaster box and collect the money and distribute it to the poor?'

*…doing something **religious** with the money!*

*…**doing the religious thing!***

That's exactly how Judas reasoned, *and **he was offended.***

*He was **indignant.***

And then what happened to him?

In the same chapter *he ended up betraying Jesus for a month's salary*.

(There is nothing wrong with becoming an engineer or a businessperson for Jesus,

*…but I am fully persuaded that every new believer, every young believer **ought to follow their heart so God can use them in the ministry,***

*…**and let every other pursuit in life become secondary to the great commission and the work of the ministry.***

Then when some of them do go on to be engineers and whatever have you, *they can be far stronger Christians and be far stronger in their witness and actually make a difference in the world around them*.)

I want you to see that, *that woman **was in love with her Savior and her God.***

And while Judas interpreted it as waist, *she was busy being used by God,*

…and God only promotes His own; the ones *who value what He values!*

She was prophesying Jesus' resurrection.

(In those days that ointment, that very costly substance was used as a final gift *from a loved one to a loved one,* to restrain the stench of death in their body.

Remember Lazarus was dead for 4 days and by that time he stank, the Bible says.)

This woman *was prophesying without even knowing,* and Jesus referred to it.

He said:

*'**Everywhere this gospel is preached, what this woman did will be told in memory of her**.'*

She prophesied that His body will not be given to decay like Lazarus's body, but *on the third day He would rise.*

My point in saying all this is that *the moment you begin to give unselfishly,* what

you do *is valued* in the spirit realm, in spirit currency.

...and it affords you *true spirit wealth* and also true spirit promotion!

...not a fleshly promotion of you,

...*but a promotion of the things of God, of the kingdom of God through you!*

Everything has natural value *and spirit value.*

What this women did *far <u>out valued</u> this alabaster box's natural value.*

She changed its natural value *into spirit value,*

...<u>she did a currency exchange</u> *when she decided to use it unselfishly in a love sacrifice to Jesus,*

When she poured it out in service to Jesus, *she tapped into the monitory system of Heaven.*

God wants us to begin to *operate* in the monitory system of Heaven, *in spirit value,* amen!

God wants us to begin to operate *in another realm,* in another currency, *under another system,*

…Heavenly currency,

*…*where moth and rust *cannot limit value* any longer,

…rustproof currency,

…rustproof living!

Can you put a price on that?

Discover *the wealth of your treasure* in the spirit realm, <u>in the heavenly realm</u>; IN GOD.

Discover *your resources* beyond decay!

…beyond waist!

Chapter 9

Fulfillment in life

Philippians 4:6-19

6 *"Have no anxiety about anything, but in everything by prayer and supplication, with thanksgiving; let your request be made known to God."*

7 *"The peace of God, which passes all understanding, will keep your heart and your mind in Christ Jesus"*

8 *"Finally brethren, whatever is true, whatever is honorable, whatever is righteous, whatever is pure, whatever is lovely, whatever is gracious, if there is any excellence, if there is anything worthy of praise, think on these things."*

10 *"I rejoice in the Lord greatly, that now at length, you have revived your concern for me. You were indeed concerned for me, but you had no opportunity"*

11 ***"Not that I complain of want, for I have learned, in whatever state I am, to be content"***

12 *"I know how to be abased, and I know how to abound, **in any and all circumstances I have learned the secret** of facing plenty, and hunger, abundance, and want."*

13 *"I can do all things **in Him who is my strength**"*

14 *"Yet it was kind of you to share in my troubles"*

15 *"And you Philippians yourselves know that in the beginning of the gospel, when I departed from Macedonia, **no church shared with me in giving and receiving, except you only.**"*

16 *"For even in Thessalonica **you sent me help once and again for my necessities.**"*

17 *"**Not that I seek the gift, but I seek the fruit that increases to your credit**"*

18 *"I have received full payment and more, I am filled, having received from Epaphroditus the gifts you sent, **a fragrant offering, a sacrifice acceptable and pleasing to God.**"*

19 *"**God shall supply all your need according to His riches in glory in Christ Jesus**"*

Philippians 4:6

6 *"Have **no anxiety about anything**…"*

He uses very strong language to say,

*"**NO** anxiety ABOUT **ANYTHING**"*

No room to now and again be anxious about real big issues,

Ha... ha... ha...

He says:

*"**NO** anxiety ABOUT **ANYTHING**"*

That means that Paul has discovered a principle in his experience of faith *that takes his life beyond anxiety.*

Paul has <u>such confidence</u> *in the provision of this love covenant that he walks in,*

...*that he knows, there is nothing that could ever come against you *to so contradict God's love covenant,

***...to so contradict God's provision in His love,* that you would ever have reason to be anxious.**

By *"NO** anxiety ABOUT **ANYTHING**"* he means that you would never be in such a unique situation, *where God's provision in Christ would fail you.***

That means, you're thinking that you've come into such a unique problem;

…I mean it is such a big problem, so unique, there's never ever been a problem like it before,

…Jesus never had that problem; the disciples never had such a problem,

…you've got this big, unique problem, *and now God Himself can't reach you in His provision.*

But I've got good news for you;

…you can rest assured; you can have *"NO anxiety ABOUT ANYTHING,"* because God *can* reach you,

*…His provision **can** reach you!*

His love covenant is unfailing!

When Paul is saying:

*"Have **NO anxiety ABOUT ANYTHING"*** he is not trying to use some kind of psychological brainwashing method *to get you to just think positively about your problem,*

…almost like someone walking on a bed of hot coals, saying:

'It's cool, it's cool, it's cool'

Ha…ha…ha…

Or like the positive thinker who found himself in hell, and said:

'It's not hot, it's not hot, it's not hot'

Ha...ha...ha...

It's amazing to me how we have reduced these mighty, mighty revelations of truth and love, this mighty, mighty principle in the Word of God, how we have reduced it, to soul-realm-things.

I thank God that the things we are dealing with *have real power behind them;*

...they are not just insignificant, insufficient, ineffective little positive confessions.

Powerful spiritual forces are behind these truths!

Almighty God is behind these truths in the Word!

He is intently engaged in these things *to enforce them!*

We are talking about being in covenant with Almighty God Himself!

Philippians 4:6 & 7

6 *"Have **NO** anxiety ABOUT **ANYTHING**,*

…instead, IN EVERYTHING by prayer and supplication (making a request based on legal rights, based on that love covenant), *with thanksgiving,*

…let your request be made known to God."

7 *"The peace of God, which passes all understanding, will keep your heart and your mind in Christ Jesus"*

You see **God wants His peace to govern your heart, not your anxiety** to govern your heart and your mind.

Those are the two target areas of the enemy, **your heart and your mind.**

They are linked.

Those are the two areas you have to guard from attack,

…by building a fortress of the Word of God around it,

…through your meditation on God's truth and on His love!

Verse 8 speaks of your meditation:

Philippians 4:8

8 *"Finally brethren,* (…Of utmost importance brethren),

…whatever is true, whatever is honorable…"

The New Testament never tells you:

'**<u>Don't</u> think about**…'

The New Testament always says to:

'**<u>THINK</u> about <u>THESE</u> things**'

Have you ever tried to un-think a thought?

How do you un-think a thought?

You can't un-think a thought.

How do you get rid of your anxiety?

You see anxiety is the fruit of a negative meditation.

You're not just anxious overnight.

You're anxious as a fruit of, as a result of meditating on the negative.

But how do you now un-think that thought?

You can't, *but you can destroy that thought, you can replace that thought.*

And that's what God wants!

How do you get rid of darkness?

By bringing in the light!

How do you get rid of the negative?

By bringing in the covenant truths of the Word!

So, the Bible never says:

*'**Don't** think about these things.'*

The Bible says:

*"**THINK** about **THESE** things."*

*"The old things have passed away, **BEHOLD** the new has come."*

BEHOLD the new!

*"**THINK about THESE things!**"*

Hallelujah!

And so Paul says:

Philippians 4:8

*8 "...whatever is honorable, whatever is righteous, whatever is pure, whatever is lovely, whatever is gracious, if there is any excellence, if there is anything worthy of praise, **THINK about THESE things.**"*

In the original Greek text one of those has to do with friendship, and I understand it to say: *'Think pro-friendship thoughts.'*

Listen never consider a thought of jealousy or strife or any other thought that would possibly ruin a relationship.

Never consider it.

Always think pro-friendship thoughts.

Philippians 4:10

10 *"I rejoice in the Lord greatly, that now at length, you have revived your concern for me..."*

You know, it's possible to have your concern *aroused,*

...to become involved with someone financially, or to become involved with someone in any possible way,

...*and it's possible to also loose that concern; to lose that love and that fondness and that care.*

But now Paul says:

*"**Finally you have revived your concern for me ...your care for me, your love for me,***

*...**I rejoice in that**..."*

Something must have happened here in this relationship.

The enemy sought to somehow separate these people from Paul.

Later on in this Scripture you can see how these people, right from the beginning; *they were partners with Paul in his ministry,*

…and somehow, through perhaps some negative report, or some criticism of Paul, or something like that, that has come to their ears,

…or maybe something else that has happened, *they have withdrawn their support and commitment to Paul.*

And now suddenly, for whatever reason, just out of the blue, *they are revived in their love and care.*

But now what is Paul saying?

He says:

Philippians 4:10

10 *"I rejoice in the Lord greatly, that now at length, you have revived your concern for me.*

…You were indeed concerned for me, but you had no opportunity…"

He's just giving them the benefit of the doubt here by saying that,

'…there just wasn't any opportunity for you to express your concern in a practical way.'

…even though it's not really true, **but he's not condemning them for it!**

In verse 11 he says:

11 *"**And I am not complaining of want**…"*

You see Paul could write this letter and say to those guys;

*'Now listen, you know, for the last six months, since I've heard that you've promised to send me a gift and your gift hasn't arrived, I've been on a six month fast, and you guys, if you think that my ministry is at least worth something, then at least send me a gift and I'll add my little envelope, you know, in the letter, for your convenience you know, so you can just send it you know, **as soon as you can**,*

*…because brothers, you know if you don't send your gifts now, **I'm going to have to close down my ministry.**'*

No, Nonsense!

He didn't say that!

What is he saying?

Philippians 4:11

11 *"Not that I complain of want **for I have learned**...*"

And if Paul has learned it, I believe we can too.

What did he learn?

11 *"...**for I have learned** in whatever state I am,*

New York, you know, Texas, South Carolina,

Ha...ha...ha...

11 *"**I have learned** in whatever state I am,*

...whether it's in the wilderness, on the mission field,

...*in the desert,*

Ha...ha...ha...

*"**TO BE CONTENT**..."*

God knows, that the only thing that makes us vulnerable to temptation, *is when we lose our sense of contentment.*

The moment you become unfulfilled in life, **you might as well know it already, *you're an open target for temptation,***

...because temptation is Satan's alternative to fulfillment in Christ!

Paul says:

"I've learned the secret to be content"

I believe learning this secret to be content is one of the most powerful secrets you can learn.

It will release you from anxiety in any world!

...whether it be first world countries, or third world countries,

...whether it be the world Paul lived in, or today's world,

...even tomorrow's world!

Sometimes we think this secret of contentment is one of just putting up with the problem, enduring through it.

It's not that.

Contentment is never just putting up with the problem.

Listen, the moment you walk in contentment, *it means you walk in the revelation of grace,*

...in the full appreciation and the full application of that grace message of God!

When you walk in the full knowledge, the full appreciation and full application of it, *it means you walk in the fullness of God's sufficiency.*

And when you walk in the fullness of God's sufficiency, *you walk in power.*

You rule over circumstances; you rule over contradiction in your life *through this contentment.*

So I say again;

...contentment is not being just weak and putting up with the problem,

...contentment is *ruling by faith* from His sufficiency,

...not His sympathy, not His pity, *His sufficiency!*

"My grace is your sufficiency" God said to Paul, in 2Corinthians 12:9.

When we discover God's grace, *it's not God's ability to put up with us,*

...or God's gift to us to put up with the devil, NO, *it is God's sufficiency.*

When we discover God's grace, we discover God's abundance, God's ability, God's strength, God's sufficiency!

And **how do I measure that sufficiency?**

I measure it in terms of *what God legally did in Christ Jesus!*

Everything God accomplished on my behalf in His Son's death and resurrection *measures His sufficiency.*

So, the secret of that contentment is the basic secret of *living free from anxiety.*

Look at what he says in verse 12:

Philippians 4:12

12 *"I know how to be abased, and I know how to abound, **in any and all circumstances I have learned the secret of facing plenty, and hunger, abundance, and want.**"*

Do you know there will be times when you will have to face hunger; *when you will have to face want?*

I am saying; there will be times when you have to face off hunger, *when you will have to have a faceoff with want.*

Experiencing hunger and want doesn't sound very prosperous *when measured in worldly standards, or measured against the American dream.*

It sounds like a foreign doctrine to those who live by the principles of the faith and prosperity message being preached in the churches today.

I mean; there was a day in Paul's life, his first prison encounter, when he really discovered the power of the wonderful doctrine of praise in all circumstances.

They sat there with their Bibles and they pulled it out and they studied the principles of spiritual warfare and Paul said to Silas:

'All right Silas, this is our day.'

And they began very reluctantly with the first hymn, you know, I mean they were sort of rather down in the dumps you know, because here they are, God's men, you know, God's missionaries landing up in prison.

'I mean they told us in Bible school, 'brothers you are going to drive a Mercedes Benz in two years, and you're going to have it made, if you really get a hold of these principles of giving and of faith and spiritual warfare, you're going to have it made, you work one day a week and the rest you just kind of visit the people, brothers there's not a better job, ministry is it!'

'And now look at us, here we are in prison, you know, ridiculed, misunderstood, we've been beaten with rods …real rods,

…and we're rather miserable about it.'

So very reluctantly Paul tested his voice to see if he can hold the right key,

Ha… ha… ha…

…and he and Silas started their song,

…and they were really like gearing it up,

Ha… ha… ha…

…and getting louder and louder in this spiritual warfare kind of thing,

…they were really getting into this principle of praise now you see, until they finally started feeling better about where they were, you see,

'Oh it's wonderful to discover the principle of praise,

…you should just try it sometime and discover its power, see for yourself, it works, you know,

…you can tear down spiritual strongholds with it you know.'

No, no, no!

The Bible doesn't say anything about them employing the principle of praise now,

…or about them entering into the principles of spiritual warfare, and tearing down so called strongholds in the heavenlies!

Acts 16:25 doesn't say they were yelling at the devil or even warring with the devil,

…it simply says,

*"…at midnight Paul and Silas were praying and singing hymns **to God**…"*

So what really happened there?

I believe there was so much covenant knowledge, so much joy in that prison, so much faith in God, so much faith in the love of God, so much faith in that love-covenant,

…there was so much strategy, so much destiny in that prison, *all wrapped up in the bosoms of these men.*

Their hearts and minds were so filled with the revelation of righteousness;

…with the revelation of their true identity in Him;

…with the revelation of their sonship and their Daddy's love for them,

...so much so, that they exploded before God in prayer, and praise and worship and adoration, *for all that has been given to them in relationship with Him, in friendship, and fellowship with Him;*

...for all that has been restored to them in Christ Jesus!

The Bible continues to say,

"... and the prisoners were listening to them."

They drew everyone in that prison into their intimate time of praise and worship they were enjoying with the Father.

It's amazing how, *when we do not understand faith and trust in relationship because of the intimacy of love,*

...how we want to make a doctrine out of everything,

...how we get so easily caught up in a principle for this, and a principle for that.

'Brother if it doesn't work when you sing it the first time, sing it ten times, and sooner or later you'll break through to heaven, you know,

...and once you've learned how to break through, brother, then all you have to do when you get in that situation again is to do the same thing,

...*and it's got to happen the same way it did the other day, and have the same results*.'

...but then it doesn't, *and we wonder why.*

We've developed all these so-called principles,

...*wanting to just exploit doctrine for our own benefit!*

And understand me now correctly; I am not saying that there are not times *when it becomes necessary for us to confess things,* **and to hold fast to our confession of faith**,

...or times where *we need to declare things in the spirit by faith,*

...but we in the charismatic world **have made a principle of everything!**

...*instead of just simply **walking in abundant** <u>**life**</u>,*

...*simply **enjoying life** more abundantly **in Him!***

...*simply enjoying **HIM!***

...*enjoying **His love for us!***

Listen, Paul learned *the real secret,*

...*the secret of abiding in HIM,*

...abiding in His eternal LOVE,

...abiding in that eternal LIFE,

...and it took his life beyond circumstance and beyond doctrine!

Philippians 4:11

11 *"I have learned in whatever state I am,*

...state hunger, or state want,

...state rejection, or state persecution,

...state prison,

...or state country,

Ha... ha... ha...

"I have learned ... to be content!"

...In other words, there's a liberty within me,

...that remains <u>unhindered</u>!

Unhindered?

Yes, <u>*unhindered!*</u>

...because I have an unhindered approach before my Father, Hallelujah!

Paul spent days and months and sometimes years, *in prison …real prison,*

…without having <u>any</u> limitation in his experience with God,

…or in his ministry,

He remained <u>secure</u> in God's love for him; *his faith never wavered.*

Paul wasn't locked up in prison for days and months, *because he lost something with God,*

…or because he had a faith problem,

…or because he just didn't understand the principles of spiritual warfare,

…or because he just didn't understand some other key principles,

No, there was nothing wrong with Paul or with his faith, amen!

Being in prison, ***didn't limit his ministry,***

…no, ***he saw it, and used it,*** *as merely* ***another opportunity,***

…just a different audience,

…just another opportunity, to reach yet another group of people with the gospel!

The impact of the Gospel of God through Paul's life *remained unfettered,*

...**unrestricted!**

...**because his experience with God remained unlimited and unhindered!**

11 *"I have learned the secret in whatever state I am* **TO BE CONTENT***..."*

That means:

...**abundance won't add encouragement, *neither will lack add disappointment.***

...**abundance can no longer add to my life; *neither can lack steal from me!***

Contentment is a completeness that you know in God:

A completeness of enjoyment in His presence, *in His intimate countenance,*

...**a satisfaction, that you've come to know, that you've come to experience constantly, through faith,**

...**through intimate fellowship,**

...***a saturating fulfillment,***

...**a complete contentment experienced *in Him,***

…because of that faith-agreement!

…because of that total agreement between me and God!

…a complete contentment experienced in Him,

…in His love,

…joy unspeakable and full of glory,

…because of righteousness;

…because of identity,

…because of sonship,

…because of my Daddy's love for me!

"Blessed are those who hunger and thirst after righteousness, **for they shall be <u>satisfied</u> (<u>filled</u>).***"*

That's the secret of contentment.

It's righteousness by faith.

Living <u>a fulfilled life</u> *in the knowledge of God's constant unchanging approval of my life!*

…in the knowledge of His eternal love for me!

...and in that contentment, *I'm in the heart of my Father,*

...and in that abiding place, *my whole life just becomes an extension of His strategy!*

And that does not mean to now put up with the devil, or to put up with principalities and powers, *but to overcome them through your righteousness,*

...*standing strong and secure in your faith,*

...*and in who you are,*

...*and in who God is to you in your life!*

We've written so many doctrines about so many things, and we've become so dogmatic in our whole Christian behavior.

If there is one thing though, which you can afford to get dogmatic about in a certain sense of the word, *it's on the doctrine of righteousness;*

...*on your redemption in Christ Jesus,*

...*on the truth of your true identity restored,*

...*on your sonship,*

...*on your value to Him,*

...*on His love for you!*

…it all comes from grasping the same concept,

…being rooted and grounded in an intimate walk with Him,

…understanding that absolute legality of your unhindered, unchanging approach to God,

…but don't limit your experience to *just a doctrine,*

…***don't limit your experience to knowledge.***

…***enter fully into faith,***

…***enter fully into that love,***

…***enter fully into that unhindered intimate love relationship!***

*…to where you literally "have **NO** anxiety **ABOUT ANYTHING**"*

Chapter 10

Ever-increasing credit

Philippians 4:11-13

11 *"I do not speak in regard to want, for I have learned, in whatever state I am, to be content"*

12 *"I know how to be abased, and I know how to abound,* **in any and all circumstances I have learned the secret of facing plenty, and hunger, abundance, and want**.*"*

13 *"I can do all things* **in Him who is my strength***"*

Now he says here in verse 14:

14 *"Yet it was kind of you to share in my troubles…"*

It's important that Paul relates to these people in such a way that he does not communicate the wrong thing,

…that he does not say to them:

'Hey listen guys, I don't need your support man; God's my source.'

I really want us to understand and discover the wisdom of Paul here.

He wasn't salary minded;

…He is not hinting for finances here,

…He lived in a covenant love relationship with God…

But I want you to note His covenant commitment, *the kind of love and sensitivity he walked in towards these people,*

*…*he doesn't want to hurt and wound these people, so there was no pull on them, you know, *just a little bit of manipulation,*

…no, there was not even some small hint of compulsion or condemnation and obligation put on them by Paul

He has known, through the months of knowing God's provision, whether it has been through a time of lack, or through a time of abundance,

…he has known God's provision, independent of their support,

*…*but he also knows that God has drawn these people into his life *for him to be a blessing to them,*

...and regardless of whatever happened in the past, *he was quick to overlook the past and to embrace them again in fellowship,*

...and he knows that if he would cut himself loose from them, *he would stop the blessings that would flow back to them.*

...so he walked in a mature, responsible, love-relationship towards the saints.

I want you to hear me clearly now, *for there has been enough wounded hearts of God's precious people through those who are God's ministers.*

Listen to me, *an independent spirit and faith is not the same thing.*

We are part of a body of believers, the body of Christ, *the family and household of God.*

No man is on an island by himself.

God has made us to need each other.

Don't walk in fear and greed, and underhanded manipulation, and usury and abuse of the brethren, *and call it faith,*

...nor walk in pride and loveless self-centered arrogance, *and call it faith*.

The prophet Elijah was yielded enough to God, *to receive provision when it came*

through crows, and then through the widow of Zarephath **in the region of Sidon.**

Sometimes we can say to someone,

…if perhaps that someone gets a little disappointed with you, and says:

'I'm no longer going to support you,'

*…*it is easy to respond to them **in an insensitive prideful way,** and say:

'Well, you're not my source, God's my source!'

Listen to me now;

God doesn't rain finances on you from the clouds.

Jesus said:

"…good measure, pressed down, shaken together, and running over shall **MEN** *(people) pour into your bosom."*

If you are one of God's ministers, *God always raises up people to support you financially.*

You don't need to try and raise them up yourself.

DON'T!

You don't need to write little speeches to people, and say:

'Boy oh boy, if you guys aren't going to support me, I don't know how we are going to make it here.'

God will raise them up.

"...a man's gift will make room for him"

If you truly are God's minister, *and not wounding or exploiting God's people;*

...if you walk in a sensitive love relationship with God, and God's people, bringing them life and fresh bread from heaven, *and treat them with sincere love,*

...*God will raise up someone to support you!*

God will send the crows, and the quail, and the manna!

He will support you!

Don't throw the crows with stones.

Don't mistreat them.

Respect them.

Treat them with love and respect!

So Paul says:

Philippians 4:14

14 *"Yet it was kind of you to share in my troubles..."*

He is taking the principle of God's provision in the context of their promise and their love and concern and care, and so he says in verse 15,

15 *"...and you Philippians yourselves know that in the beginning of the gospel..."*

That's not in the beginning when the gospel began, in terms of, you know, *the thought of God,* but in terms of Paul's ministry.

So He says,

"...in the beginning of my ministry..."

He was still unknown.

There was a lot of negative talk about this young man, Paul.

A lot of people thought,

'...man this guy is a conman at best,

...he's not a part of the Jerusalem church, you know; he's not part of the apostles of old; Paul's one of these new guys, he's just one of these independents you know.'

So there was a lot of talk and rumors spread about Paul.

You can read the book of Acts yourself to discover all that.

They didn't quite trust him.

There was a lot of suspicion around Paul.

But these Philippians, *they were some of the first people that were so impacted through Paul's life and ministry,* **that they were drawn into a partnership and friendship together** *in their fellowship with Paul.*

Philippians 4:15

15 *"…and you Philippians yourselves know that in the beginning of my ministry, when I departed from Macedonia, no church* **shared** *with me* **in giving and receiving,** *except you only."*

They were so impacted in their hearts through fellowship with Paul, and by his ministry of the Word to them, *that they were drawn into a partnership and friendship with Paul in ministry*;

…they were drawn into a partnership together *"in giving,"*

…and in what? …**in** *"receiving"*

A Partnership is never a one-way affair:

"...in giving and receiving."

Philippians 4:16

16 *"For even in Thessalonica you sent me help once again for my necessities"*

And now he says again in verse 17, **and this is so important:**

17 *"Not that I seek the gift..."*

When you write to your friends, when you share with people, *make very sure that you're not seeking the gift.*

I guarantee that the moment you begin to see a cow, *and you want to milk this cow,*

...it's going to put a strain on your relationship with that person.

The very moment you do it.

So DON'T go there!

Make very sure that your ministry *is never ever motivated by your need;*

...that the letter you write to people, is never motivated by lack.

This is a very powerful principle of faith and practice.

The enemy will snare you *into a slave mentality, into a beggarly mentality,* if you start employing those misguided tactics *as a means to try and muster up support.*

Faith does not work like that!

Faith does not work by hints.

Philippians 4:17

17 *"Not that I seek the gift,*

...but what do I seek?

...I seek THE FRUIT that increases to your credit."

Paul loved God's people, *he always, in love, preferred the brethren.*

Paul knew that in them continuing their partnership, their covenant, in fellowship with him, *the credit to their account continues,*

...because in their free-will giving of their substance, *they are boldly declaring their support, and so their identification with his life and ministry!*

…and in their withholding the gift, they are boldly, just as boldly, *in spirit realm,* even if nobody else knows about it, saying:

'I am no longer identifying myself with his ministry; **I no longer agree with Paul's message!***'*

…and they are going to lose out *as far as their credit is concerned,* in the heavenly bank account,

…as far as their credibility before God,

…and Paul's love for these people did not want that for them.

Philippians 4:17

17 *"…**I seek THE FRUIT which increases to your credit**."*

He says in verse 18

18 *"I have received **full payment <u>and more</u>**…"*

Did you know that living by the salary system mentality *would limit your income?*

I know of ministries in other nations that have stopped operating on the salary system altogether *…in fact there are many ministries in the third world, in other nations, that don't operate on the salary system.*

…they operate on *the faith system,*

…they operate on *the truth and love system,*

…they operate on *that system of God that is linked to the genuineness of heart,*

…*to the genuineness of faith,*

…*to the genuineness of love*

When those ministries got set free, *in their hearts, to walk in faith and love,*

…and stopped operating on the salary system ***mentally,***

…*they had a tremendous increase in their income,*

…*and an explosion in projects that they could never ever have budgeted for* under the salary system

Looking at their financial books will blow your mind, because their books never float,

…when you add it all up together, there just isn't enough money there in their day to day budget to be able to do what they are doing,

…and yet they are doing it, *because they have tapped into the grace of God!*

…they tapped into *the secret law of true enrichment of the heart, because of revelation, because of God's love towards them, that now lives in them,*

…and they are now a living testimony to the success of *God's love and faith system,*

…just like Jesus and the disciples were living testimonies of it.

I'm not going to go there right now in this book, but you can go and study for yourself *how Jesus and the disciples lived,*

…how God raised up provision for them in ministry,

…and how Jesus commanded the disciples to live, once He started sending them out in ministry.

They never suffered lack,

…and even when it seemed that way, *God always came through with a miracle.*

Jesus even needed an administrator in his ministry, and appointed Judas Iscariot *to be treasurer for them and carry the moneybag,*

…so that means they must have had plenty at times!

Let's return to Philippians.

Philippians 4:18

18 *"I have received* **full payment** **and more**, *I am filled, having receive from Epaphroditus the gifts you sent,* **a fragrant offering, a sacrifice acceptable and pleasing** *to God."*

…yet another opportunity to discover the *"MORE"* measure!

Again, it was not the gifts that *"filled"* Paul;

…it wasn't the gifts they sent that was his *"full payment* **and more***."*

What *"filled"* him; **what pleased him most**

…was *"THE FRUIT that increased to their credit;"*

…**the blessing now released to them,** **by partnering with his ministry.**

Do you see Paul's wisdom?

If he was walking in pride, he probably would have had every reason to say to them:

'Hey listen man, you have offended me; or hey listen man, I thought you were still offended at me, why change your tune now all of a sudden?'

He could have said:

'I don't need your gift, God is my source!'

But no, *he continues to desire,*

"THE FRUIT that increases to their credit,"

…so he joyfully accepts their gift as *"a pleasing sacrifice to God."*

You know, we are **a New Testament priesthood**, *and there are only three kinds of sacrifices that we can offer to God.*

The one is found in Romans 12:1,

1 *"…presenting your body, **a living** sacrifice…"*

The other is found in Hebrews 13:15,

15 *"…let us continually offer **the sacrifice of praise** to God, **the fruit of our lips**…giving thanks"*

And the **giving of our substance** is the third sacrifice.

Those are the only sacrifices that the New Testament priesthood can bring.

If there is more I haven't found it.

Maybe there is more, so don't be mad at me if you find another one,

Ha… ha… ha…

Chapter 11

Make decisions with your heart, not your head!

Philippians 4:18

18 *"I have received **full payment** __and more__, I am **filled**, having receive from Epaphroditus the gifts you sent, **a fragrant offering, a sacrifice acceptable and pleasing to God**."*

Love wants to give.

Let's go to 2Corinthinas 9:6-11

6 *"The point is this: He, who sows sparingly, will also reap sparingly, but he, who sows bountifully, will also reap bountifully."*

7 *"Each one must do **as he has made up his heart,** not reluctantly, or under compulsion, for God loves a cheerful* (happy to do it) *giver."*

8 *"God is able to provide you with **every** blessing **in abundance**, so that, always having **enough of everything**; you may also then **share abundantly** in every good work"*

9 *"As it is written: 'He scatters abroad, he gives to the poor; his righteousness endures forever.'*

(This speaks of God's Character, His love nature, His being, who He is as a person.)

And now Paul says,

10 *"He, who supplies seed to the sower, and bread for food,* **will supply, and multiply, your resources,** *and also increase the harvest of your righteousness."*

11 *"***you will be enriched in every way** (the law of true enrichment) **for great liberality and generosity***..."*

2Corinthians 9:6

6 *"***The point is this:** *He, who sows sparingly, will also reap sparingly,* **but HE, WHO SOWS BOUNTIFULLY, WILL ALSO REAP BOUNTIFULLY***..."*

Do you know that sowing and reaping is a law that God ordained. *It is part of the secret rules of true enrichment.*

God ordained the law of sowing and reaping way back in Genesis 8:22

22 *"As long as the earth remains* **seed time and harvest time will remain**.*"*

God has introduced **the law of multiplication** *through the law of sowing*.

These are laws that every farmer understands.

Whether he understands it scientifically or not, *he understands its practical benefit,* that **when you plant one seed, *there is a sure harvest that will be multiplied, beyond the number of just that one seed.***

You can count the seeds in the pumpkin, *but you cannot count the pumpkins in the seed.*

2Corinthians 9:6

6 *"**The point is this:** He, who sows sparingly, will also reap sparingly, **but HE, WHO SOWS BOUNTIFULLY, WILL ALSO REAP BOUNTIFULLY...**"*

Now let's just look at the measure that Paul uses here.

What measures *sparingly?*

...and what measures *bountifully?*

I believe the principles of tithing and giving under the Law *measures sparingly*

...and the principle of the new creation, *of the restored love nature,*

...**that principle of *love and faith* under the New Covenant *measures bountifully*.**

Because we have, for so long, emphasized the principles of tithing and giving under the Law, *we are perpetuating a vicious cycle in the Church,*

...and we have no one to blame but ourselves *for the sparing measure we are forced to cope with in ministry time and again,*

...when we could have enjoyed *a bountiful measure,* **had we only emphasized the new creation; *the restored love nature,***

...**the <u>love</u> and <u>faith</u> system of the New Covenant!**

I have seen many church projects, where, because of their teaching of the principles of tithing and giving under the Law, *they were forced to involve themselves in large financial debts,*

...and so, immediately, *their ministry **emphasis,** even more so,* became tithing and giving,

...*because the people just had to perform financially now in order to meet that monthly debt!*

...and yet, it still ended up not being enough to finish the project!

168

And so you see, the moment the Law and it's principles on tithing and giving *becomes <u>emphasized</u>* in ministry, yet again,

…reluctance follows, yet again,

…and so <u>greater legalism sets in</u>,

…and dead religion sets in, even more.

…and pretty soon that church is dead in the water!

Many have been driven from Church, by this emphasis on money because of anxiety,

…and so the Church today *has developed a negative reputation of greed* in the world we live in.

'I don't go to that church, because I feel like all they ever want is my money. It seems like the most important time of every meeting is taking up the tithe and offerings'

There are many people, who think this way,

…and can we really blame them?

They have seen right through the religious facade!

The church leaders, and leading folks in the church, may have deceived themselves through what they are doing, *but truth has a way of being revealed through the mouth of babes.*

It is to the Church's shame that we hear them say these things,

…for they are pointing out things in the Church's mindset, and the Church's actions, that should not be there.

2Corinthians 9:7 says:

*7 "Each one must do **as he has made up <u>his heart</u>**…"*

When it comes to giving, *I'd much rather listen to my heart than to my head.*

Let your heart govern your finances and your giving, *not your head.*

'Brother Rudi, the Bible says:

"Be ye transformed by the renewing of your MIND"

Yes, it does, **but it has got to be revelation in your heart first.**

It doesn't first go to your head, *and then to your heart.*

It first speaks to your heart, *and then to your head.*

Listen to what I am saying.

I have heard a lot of teaching on this, *and even believed that way myself at one point,*

...that somehow the renewing of the mind *was something that I had to* **do**,

...that; as I just gather the Scriptures together and memorize them,

...that **eventually** it will just drop from my head to my heart,

...**and suddenly** my mind will be renewed.

It's not Scriptural that way; *it only turns into legalism that way.*

The Bible says:

*"**BE YE** transformed by the renewing of your mind"*

...or more accurately,

*"**BE YE renewed in the spirit** of your mind."*

That means *you cannot renew your mind,*

*...you have to "**BE renewed in the spirit**," in order to be renewed in your mind.*

The renewing of the mind *is the direct result of the impact of the Word upon your heart.*

It takes revelation in your spirit to renew your mind.

You see it's only the Word of faith *that quickens your faith,* and so renews your mind.

Otherwise you just become theological and legalistic!

That's why many people can know the doctrine of such and such, and the doctrine of this and that, *because they know it in their heads.*

But it's *once your heart is embraced of truth and by love* that your mind is automatically renewed.

You see God is a God that speaks *a heart language,*

God speaks *heart to heart.*

He desires to communicate <u>love</u>, *not principle and doctrine,*

...and so through the intimate truth of His love in your heart, *touching your heart, embracing your heart,* your mind is renewed

So make up your mind *by determining in your heart.*

You can only make up your mind *with your heart.*

In Hosea 11 there is a beautiful Scripture of how God's mind has to execute His fierce anger, and in the very next verse, verse 8 God says:

*"My **heart** recoils within me. How can I give you up **when my compassion grows warm and tender?**"*

(Go read it for yourself in the RSV Translation; it is an absolutely beautiful prophetic picture.)

He says:

*"...**My compassion grows worm and tender.** I cannot execute my fierce anger"*

A moment ago God's mind and God's justice said:

'Israel must be condemned, because they are stubborn of heart. They refuse to listen to me.'

BUT he says:

"My heart recoils within me, my compassion is stirred, and it grows warm and tender"

And I believe there in Hosea 11 God saw His son's death,

…God was already looking at His Son's death on our behalf and His heart grew warm and tender.

I know I got a little bit sidetracked by this, *but it's still the same principle.*

Let your heart make up your mind.

Never determine what to do with your finances, or what to give, *with your legalistic mind,*

…determine with your heart.

2Corinthians 9:7

7 *"Each one must do **as he has made up his heart**, not reluctantly, or under compulsion, for God loves a cheerful* (happy to do it) *giver…"*

*"…**for God loves a cheerful giver**…"*

If we study cheerful giving, *we must first discover what releases that joy,*

…because the only alternative is, reluctant giving

Listen, Man can be motivated to do anything, *through reward, or through punishment.*

In 1Peter 5:2 Peter speaks from this principle, to the elders and the spiritual leadership in the Church, and he says:

2 *"Tend the flock of God that is in your charge,* **not by constraint, <u>but willingly,</u> not for shameful gain, <u>but eagerly.</u>** *"*

"Willingly" and *"***eagerly***"* is just another definition of this same principle of *cheerful giving*.

When I do something under *"***constraint***,"* or *"***reluctantly***"* it means, I'm just doing it by law and legalism, and fear of punishment.

…it means, I am not doing it **from the heart;**

…I'm not doing it, **with a genuine heart!**

When I do something *"***for shameful gain***"* or *"***under compulsion***,"* I am motivated to do it, *because I know there's going to be some reward for me, and I'm looking for that reward.*

But God has another motivation in mind for us to live by.

2Corinthians 9:8 & 9

8 *"God is able to provide you with* **every (spiritual, and therefore, every natural) blessing <u>in abundance</u>***"*

(That's the **much more** of the gospel),

*"…so that, **always having enough of everything**,"*

(…he is talking about having enough true spiritual enrichment and fulfillment, *which makes whatever you have in the natural enough, whether you have plenty at the moment or not so plenty, but it is enough, you see it as enough, you see it as abundance, because of that spiritual abundance you walk in,* and so) *"…**you may share abundantly in every good work**."*

9 *"As it is written: 'He scatters abroad, he gives to the poor; **his righteousness endures forever**.'*

Did you know that your righteousness, *your joy, your enjoyment of God's intimate covenant relationship of truth and love with you,* is made manifest in your giving?

10 *"He, who supplies seed to the sower, **and bread for food**…"*

(He is talking about the seeds of righteousness, which becomes spiritual bread that feeds the hearts of the hearers;

…he is not just talking about natural resources and food like bread. He says,)

*"He, who supplies seed to the sower, **and bread for food**…"*

He is quoting Isaiah 55, where Isaiah asks in the previous verses:

*"Why do you weigh out your money, for that which is not **true bread?**"*

So he goes on to say here:

2Corinthians 9:10

10 *"He, who supplies seed to the sower, and bread for food, **will supply and multiply your resources**"*

*"…**and increase the harvest of your righteousness!**"*

Hallelujah!

11 *"…**you will be enriched <u>in every way</u> for great liberality and generosity!**"*

(He is talking about the law of true enrichment and fulfillment; *he is talking about righteousness being in operation*)

God wants SEED and BREAD *to be your portion.*

One of the first principles that I learned in ministry was, *the Word of Righteousness; the Word of my Identity and sonship and faith,*

…and then the second principle that I learned, which goes right along with that, *was the seed and bread principle,*

…and I am quite sure that, if God did not teach me that principle of identity and sonship and faith, and the seed and bread principle, that goes right along with that, *I would not have survived in ministry.*

Listen; there is a difference between seed and bread.

You can't eat your seed.

Spiritual or natural, *everything you have is either seed or bread.*

Even what was bread has to become seed as well!

So, don't cling to it for yourself only, *and hold on to it too long!*

Don't let it go to waist, *rather turn it into seed!*

Bread speaks of that which satisfies me, and it speaks also of my now needs.

Things that I need right now, like a bed to sleep on, or clothes to wear,

…that which God has provided for me for the now.

But in all that I have *there is seed.*

I had to begin to change my attitude towards my possessions.

Where before, I thought that everything I had was bread, but now God said:

'I want you to start to learn the responsibility of sowing. **You can only eat so much bread a day.**

Instead of storing the rest, storing what you are not using,

…and sometimes even if you are still using it,

…sow it!

…it's your best investment!*'*

Your best investment is to sow!

And so I began to practice it on a daily basis, *as an act of my generous love nature,*

…as something I live by.

God showed me, how tithing would actually serve *to limit my love and faith,*

…and it would then also limit the flow of the Spirit,

…*and the flow of His generous love nature through me,*

…*and also then the abundance of His provision in my life,*

…*because it is attached to that flow!*

God will always provide for me in my life!

…but the abundant flow of that provision in my life *is directly attached to that flow of God's Spirit in my life,*

…and to the flow of His generous love nature, into me and through me,

…to the flow of everything that comes to me from Him, and then flows through my life to others!

As I said before:

Tithing can only release you *into a limited measure of liberty and provision.*

I saw how tithing would keep me bound to *the whole reluctance of having to give religiously,*

…you know, counting my pennies,

…and, *'Ugh, nine I can have for myself, you know, without sweat, but one I have got to give away to God.'*

Tithing was a principle of education under the Law, *for a people that were fallen in their thinking and mindset, and therefore their tendencies, their nature.*

It was their nature to *hold*,

*…**but it is our nature to <u>give</u>!***

But God began to motivate me, **to take everything I have *and share it, in love, with others,***

*…***<u>everything</u>, even my privacy!***

*…and I began to reap, **in abundance!***

There were often times, when I needed a specific sum of money, *and God would give me the seed, and let me know that it is seed, and that He is making my sowing part of the solution, and a part of the provision and the abundance He was about to release to me…*

I want to teach you this **as a revelation.**

When you need $300.00 and God gives you $30.00 or $10.00,

…don't store it until you have $300.00.

What you were given is not bread, *it is seed.*

Trust God and sow it in love to someone else.

If you need a full tank of gas to get to where you need to go to, but you only have $5.00, *don't throw in $5.00 and see how far you can go on $5.00*

*…**No**, you threw your seed away; you ate your seed.*

Sow it!

…**that's your seed!**

…and I am not trying to turn these precious principles into yet another law and get you to become all legalistic about it,

…**just be sensitive,**

…**listen to God's voice,**

…**and go with His lead,**

…**and be free in the love of God**!

…but I want you to know that these principles I am talking about *have everything to do **with revelation knowledge,***

…***with faith and trust in God,***

…a generous spirit *is born form the revelation **that He loves me and that I can trust Him,***

…and therefore I can be myself, my new creation self, not my stingy fearful greedy old self, *but my generous liberated self, designed for, and released by God,* **to walk in His very own generous love nature!**

Do you even know how we have limited ourselves, *just by living with our seed?*

God wants you to live with your bread only.

Sow your seed.

God wants you to live in harvest provision.

I'm telling you, it is one of the most liberating and bountiful things you can ever enter into in your life, *to let your love and faith rule,*

…to live *free* **even financially,**

…*to live on your bread <u>only</u>*

…*and to keep sowing your seed!*

There is nothing I know of in the natural *that can liberate you more* than to stop having to count your pennies and hold on to it for dear life, and *'O God, what are we going to do tomorrow?'*

Have you ever seen a bird *worry* about tomorrow's worms?

Having a heart attack, a panic attack:

'O, I can't stand it, it looks like it's going to be cloudy weather, and that means we're going to have no worms, and it's rainy and cold and miserable, and we're going to have no worms, because the worms are all going to hide in the ground.'

God wants to release you *when you discover His love and His provision.*

Can you see that behind your sowing *is a resource that is much larger than your $5.00?*

You might only have $5.00 in your pocket, *but you have a wealth of knowledge in your heart, that far out measures your need.*

...and God wants that knowledge of God and of who we really are as His kids to grow in our spirit and to so impact our heart until we base our faith, not on believing God for $20.00,

...*but we're basing our faith on love,*

...*on the immeasurable wealth of the gift of God in Christ Jesus,*

When you're basing your faith on His love, *and His covenant provision already given you in that love,*

...you'll find that you never ever need to believe God again for financial needs, or for health even.

When your faith is rooted and grounded in the knowledge of God's love and provision,

...in the knowledge of His superabundance,

...you'll know the secret of living a content life, a fulfilled life,

...a life with enough faith for any situation,

*...*you'll learn the secret of facing plenty, and facing want.

You'll face it with a confidence of God's love and provision <u>that far out-measures your need</u>.

When you discover that He, who supplies breed for food, *is also the one, who supplies seed for sowing,*

*...*you will soon discover that, *sowing is much more exciting than eating,*

...much more exciting!

Imagine a life that is reduced to just sustaining the flesh,

*...*you know, just eating as much meat as I can get, and as much veggies, and as much soda,

and all the nice things, *and I'm just going to eat and eat and eat,*

…I mean, **your life will be *such a boar,***

…you'll be so fat soon, *you'll pop!*

Ha…ha…ha…

God wants us to discover sowing, *in terms of His own initiative.*

John 3:16

16 *"**God <u>so very much loved</u> the world <u>that He gave</u> His Son, begotten only of God…"***

He sowed *when apparently there was no bread left!*

…and He gave Him who is the bread from Heaven.

He gave His Son, *His own Son.*

"…unless a Seed falls into the ground and dies, it remains alone; but if it dies, it produces much fruit."   - John 12:24

In Genesis 26 we read how Isaac *wants to hop out of the land, because there is famine in the land of promise.*

'This move we made here to this supposed land of promise cannot be God, you know,

because I don't see the abundance of His promise, I don't see it, maybe we just misinterpreted God, it could be that maybe it's actually Egypt that God had in mind,'

'...and so I've got my little lunch bag ready, my only provision, you see, perhaps one more bag of seed, and there is going to be enough bread,

...I mean, I will have enough for the road you know, and when we get there I can just sow my little bit in Egypt,

...and pray a little bit,

...and then maybe we can make a living in Egypt.'

God says:

*"Do not go down to Egypt; **sow in this land**."*

*"Isaac sowed **in that land** and in that same year (the year of famine), **reaped a hundredfold**."*

God never ever wants you to be limited, amen!

It's your faith in Him,

...and your sowing from that faith, that now releases you from any temporal prison that seeks to hold you, and confine you, to your need.

Chapter 12

Living beyond your means

2Corinthians 8:1-5

1 *"We want you to know brethren, about the grace of God, which has been shown in the churches of Macedonia"*

2 *"for, in a severe test of affliction, **their abundance of joy, in spite of their extreme poverty, have overflowed, in a wealth of liberality on their part.**"*

3 *"For they gave, according to their means, as I can testify, **and beyond their means, <u>by their own free will</u>**,"*

4 *"**begging us earnestly for the favor of taking part, in ministering to the needs of the saints**"*

5 *"...**and this they did,** beyond our expectation; **they first gave themselves to the Lord, by the will of God, and then to us also.**"*

2Corinthians 8:1

1 *"We want you to know brethren, about the grace of God, **which has been shown** in the churches of Macedonia…"*

Did you know that you can make the grace of God visible?

You can make the grace of God *more than a doctrine.*

You can make it *evident* for people *to behold, and experience, in the most practical way possible, <u>through your life</u>*.

And what is the grace of God?

Everything that God did for us in Christ.

You can make everything God did for Man in Christ *so visible, so practical, that no one can miss it.*

2 *"for, in a severe test of affliction, **their abundance of joy**, in spite of their extreme poverty, <u>**have overflowed**</u> in a wealth of liberality on their part."*

Did you know that tests of affliction will come your way?

2 *"…in a **severe** test of affliction…"*

You see you get affliction, and AFFLICTION.

When the Word speaks of the Christian armor in Ephesians 6 it speaks of being,

*"...able to stand **in the evil day**..."*

There are some days *that are even more evil,*

...where the attack is more severe than in other days,

*...but then, in the midst of that situation, God makes provision for you, **through His truth that the Holy Spirit within you reminds you of**, and you overcome.*

In 2Peter 1:3 he says:

*"**He has granted to us <u>all things</u>** that pertain to life and godliness"*

So He has obviously made provision *for the most sever affliction that you can ever encounter*.

When someone designs a vehicle and he places a little sticker on the vehicle that says: **4x4**,

...then that vehicle is obviously designed to drive in areas where a normal vehicle would not perform that well.

There are certain things built into that vehicle, so that when you want to use your 4x4 to go up a mountain somewhere, and down a valley, and through a ditch, *you'll not get stuck in the mud.*

That vehicle is designed to take that extreme test.

It doesn't mean that you <u>only</u> drive there, *but it's nice to know that you can handle it when a situation arises that call for it.*

There are times when you don't need to draw from all the features that are built into that vehicle,

…but there are times where circumstances arise in the road up ahead, that present a test to that vehicle, *where you can confidently draw upon all the features built into that 4x4 truck.*

You don't need to sit there and sweat and worry, *'how am I going to get through the desert?'*

You've got it all right there, *built into the vehicle already.*

And so, **God wants us to discover that He has given to us *His faith deposit in us*,**

…and with it, *every possible thing that we would ever need* to live this life in superabundance.

God says in the Psalms, *"I will give you deer's feet"*

That's how you turn a mountain into a highway, *with deer's feet.*

You know those mountain goats, found in the Colorado Mountains and elsewhere, *even the little ones, from the youngest to the oldest, they've got special shoes on man, and they don't slip on slippery places,*

…I mean, they run with the greatest of ease up the steepest cliffs.

That's how God turns mountains into highways.

Hallelujah!

He gives you the secret of facing severe affliction even.

Hallelujah.

So when affliction is there <u>in full volume</u>, *what is my protection?*

…*my, "abundance of joy!"*

I'm telling you now, if the enemy *can affect your joy,* he can overcome you with affliction.

The moment you start responding *like a mere man* to any contradiction that comes to you in life, *that contradiction will overcome you.*

The first place it will overcome you *is in your mind and in your tongue,*

...you'll start thinking and talking as if God doesn't love you,

...and as if God's covenant isn't real,

...and as if Jesus never died,

...and suddenly you'll start talking the greatness of your problem,

...and the thing will overcome you.

But, **the way you overcome the severe test of affliction is, with an** *"abundance of joy."*

Where do you get that *"abundance of joy"* from?

From the knowledge *of faith;*

...from the knowledge **which faith brings to you!**

So, there's a constant drawing *from the faith reservoir,*

...from that strength that we have in our Father's love,

...from that strength that we have in His presence!

What a strength we have **in Him!**

*"In his presence **there** is **fullness** of joy."*

2Corinthians 8:1-2

1 *"We want you to know brethren, **about the grace of God,** which has been shown in the churches of Macedonia"*

2 *"for, in a severe test of affliction, **their abundance of joy,** in spite of their extreme poverty, **have overflowed** in a wealth of liberality on their part."*

So he says that the severe test of affliction was *an extreme poverty* that faced them.

The severe test of affliction could be anything,

…but in this situation it was an extreme poverty.

They've had their last bit of rice and pancake and baked beans, and that was it.

So what did they do?

'Well brothers, let's go and intercede, I mean, we're in a good position to fast now, because we've got no food, so, let's seek God,

…and let's just seek into our hearts, to see if there's not some hidden sin somewhere,

…because here we are, and we ran out of food!

O, what a tragedy has befallen us!

…someone in the camp must have sinned, God is mad at us.'

Listen to me;

…if the devil can get you to believe that way he'll keep you poor in every way, not just financially.

How did they respond to their need?

They responded with an *"**abundance of joy**."*

And you know what they did?

They didn't say,

'Well brethren we're going through a difficult time now, we're just going to have to count our coins and just see how much we've got and hold on to it, you know,

…and just try and, oh, we're going to have to just pray hard you know,

…and I tell you what, we're going to just stop our normal program, and pray the whole day, and pray the whole night, and fast, and really hold on to the promises of God,

196

…and brother so-and-so, you confess Philippians 4:19,

…and you sister so-and-so, confess this one,

…and you, you confess that one,

…and, you know, we'll just carry on confessing, holding on to the promises of God for dear life,

…and then maybe God will stop being mad at us, and finally hear from Heaven, and have mercy on us.

…we'll just keep pounding the gates of Heaven, until this season is over,

…and then, praise God, we can finally go on with our normal program again.'

"*Abundance of joy*" doesn't speak that way!

"*The righteousness of faith*" doesn't speak that way!

That's abundance of anxiety made manifest in a very religious way.

So, what did they do?

How did they respond to their need?

Paul says that their "*abundance of joy*" <u>**overflowed**</u> **their extreme poverty,**

*"…**in a wealth of liberality**"*

2Corinthians 8:3

3 *"**For they gave,** according to their means…"*

I want you to clearly see that *there are different degrees of giving.*

The principle of tithing under the Law is a certain degree, a certain measure of giving, *a limited degree, and a limited measure!*

…meant for the lawless to convict them in their actions,

…for the rebellious to condemn them in their disobedience

It is meant for people *who do not yet live by the law of Christ;*

…by the law of faith and love and trust!

…it is meant for those who still have no understanding of New Testament truths,

…it is meant for those who have no understanding of New Covenant realities,

…of righteousness and of sonship!

The Law is not meant **for sons**, *but for outsiders and foreigners.*

Matthew 17:24-27

24 *"And when they had come to Capernaum, those who received the temple tax came to Peter and said, 'Does your Teacher not pay the temple tax?'*

25 *"He said, 'Yes.' And when he had come into the house, Jesus already anticipated him, and said to him, '**What do you think, Simon? From whom do the kings of the earth take customs or taxes, from their own sons, or from strangers?**'*

26 *"Peter said to Him: 'From strangers.' So Jesus said to him, '**Then the sons are free!**'*

27 *'NEVERTHELESS, LEST WE OFFEND THEM, go to the sea, cast in a hook, and take the first fish you snag. And when you have opened its mouth, you will find a piece of money (a coin called a shekel, the exact temple tax amount for two people); take that and give it to them for Me and you."*

Listen, Jesus came to elevate us above law *into a greater measure of freedom,*

…the freedom of sons!

We are sons, you see, *not servants,*

…*but by introducing the freedom of righteousness, the freedom of sonship, *He is also introducing a greater measure of

love and responsibility than what the Law requires.

We are drawn into *a greater measure of love and devotion* than what is usually required of servants.

Taxes are a minimum requirement imposed on strangers and foreigners,

...but righteousness, sonship, *draws us into a greater measure of responsibility because of love,*

...even though it holds a greater measure of liberty!

You see <u>a whole lot more love</u> is expressed *between a son and a father,*

...than between an owner and a slave

The level of love, dedication, devotion and sacrifice *a son is drawn into through a father's love* <u>is much greater</u> than that of strangers and foreigners and servants.

A son's whole life is wrapped up in family business where only a mere tax is required of strangers and foreigners.

Jesus did not come to undo that which the Law was trying to implement and establish,

...He came to complete the Law; *He came to fulfill the righteous requirements of the Law,*

...He came to implement the very thing the Law was trying to prepare us for;

...*He came to introduce the substance of what the Law was only a shadow of.*

Now don't write people off who still live by *a limited measure of giving,*

...a lesser degree of giving

Don't wound or bring a stumbling block to those who are still babes in Christ and need the discipline of tithing in their lives *until they learn to live by a bigger measure, a higher law, the law of Christ, the law of faith, the law of love and generosity.*

Don't go back to your church now and say,

'Pastor, you guys are still in bondage if you're still tithing.'

That's their measure of faith, *so honor that,*

...bless them in their practice of tithing; *there is nothing wrong with tithing.*

Paul warned us *to prefer our brethren and not to argue with them* that are still weak **in the faith**

…note that neither I, nor Paul, call those people weak.

Paul meant that *they can be further strengthened in faith,* that's all he is saying.

They may have many strong points, much strength, *but they need to be further strengthened,*

…just like with Apollos, *who was already strong, but needed to be strengthened some more* by Aquila and Priscilla, *through greater insight and revelation* (Acts 18:24-28, see also Romans 1:11, 12)

We are not to be the agents of strife and division, lest we become tools in the hands of the enemy, *and destroy the work of God.*

God has called us to walk in love and to protect the unity of the Spirit in the bond of peace.

Paul also said that,

*"…each servant, to his own master he stands or falls, but I tell you, **he will be made to stand, for God himself is able to make him stand**."*

If you are unable to bring edification, exhortation and comfort to the body of Christ, *then rather shut your mouth!*

Don't try and straighten people out through rebuke and insensitive correction!

...don't try and be some Old Covenant prophet!

Leave the heart surgery to real New Testament ministers, and let the foundations be restored, or relayed, by the New Testament apostles and prophets, *skilled in bringing careful adjustment to the body of Christ,*

...careful not to wound and offend, but bring insight and understanding,

...skilled in walking in the nurture, care, and love of the Lord

If you don't have enough skill, *don't mess with the foundations and bring the whole building down.*

Everybody wants to be a prophet or an apostle these days, *but **real** New Testament prophets and apostles **are not rebellious,***

...going around and destroying churches,

...and spreading their destructive habits to would-be-disciples, and up-and-coming young ministers.

Paul says,

*"According to the grace of God that was given to me, **as a wise master builder,** I have laid a foundation…"* — 1Corinthians 3:10

He also says in that same chapter,

"…each one's work will be tested to see what sort it is"

To get a better grip of how we are to act towards our brothers and sister *that we consider to be weaker **in faith** than we are,*

…you would do well to go and read Romans 13:14 all the way through till chapter 15:16,

…as well as 1Corinthians 8:1-13; 10:14-11:1 & 16,

…also 2 Thessalonians 3:3-15; and 1Timothy 1:3-11, and 6:3-4, and 20-21,

…also 2Timothy 2:14 & 23

As for me, I believe God has called me *to bring revelation,* to have an apostolic and prophetic voice to the body of Christ, to blow a trumpet with a refreshing new sound in the body of Christ, *the sound of grace!*

…the sound of accurate New Testament truth and love as it was revealed in Jesus Christ, by Father God Himself!

That new sound, that refreshing sound of the original apostolic revelation *must be heard afresh in the body of Christ.*

I don't want to see my brethren trapped in old wineskins, living in their limited measure, in their limited faith, living in their limited freedom, living in their limited blessing, living in their limited witness,

...satisfied with the wine they have been used to, *when there is more,*

...when there is better, a greater measure, a greater revelation, an unlimited freedom,

...a place of "...*good measure, pressed down, shaken together and running over,*"

...a place of "*abundant life*" and "*abundance of joy*"

It is time for the bride of Christ to be made more spotless and without blemish or shortcoming **through insight and revelation**

...so we can shine forth to a crooked and perverse generation in the full light and glory of what God has revealed concerning us and them in Christ Jesus!

It is time for us to impart greater strength to the army of the Lord, *so that we may arise in the brightness of Truth and defeat our enemies* (spiritual enemies, *not people,*) *and trample them underfoot;*

…God's enemies, our enemies, the accuser of the brethren, the father of lies, the forces of darkness and deception must be defeated and all their influence undone, they must be made His footstool by us the Church.

So, I say again, we are defeating spiritual enemies, we are not fighting with people, so don't condemn people, don't write them off if they still live by a lesser revelation, if they still live by the principle of tithing as the thing God requires of them.

Don't go back to your church and tell the Pastor that he is putting people in bondage if he still preaches tithing.

If it wasn't for tithing, *many people will never ever learn how to give.*

People can only walk in the light they have, *so don't condemn them, that's their level of faith they walk in, that's their level of revelation.*

At least they are walking in some measure of faith, at least they are walking in some measure of revelation, so bless them in their tithing,

…but don't leave them there, encourage them to go beyond their tithe, **if you can**, ***without***

fighting over it and causing strife and division.

I'm telling you now, if you go and sow discord and disunity among the brethren, *and destroy the faith of the weak ones in the process, and the work of God,* **God is not going to be pleased with you.**

Heed Paul's warning!

1Corinthians 3:17

17 *"If anyone defiles, or destroys, the temple of God,* **God will destroy him.** *For the temple of God is holy,* **which temple you all are together."**

So, there are different measures and different degrees of giving.

The Bible says there, back in 2Corinthians 8

2Corinthians 8:3

3 *"For they gave according to their means as I can testify* **and beyond their means, by their own free will…"**

This is the measure of New Covenant giving.

You finally go beyond tithing, when you give according to your means *and beyond*

your means by your own free will, _because of love_, not because of some requirement.

Listen; when there is a severe test of affliction, _you're going to have to come against that affliction with severe joy, with severe liberality_.

Do you hear by the Spirit what I am saying to you now?

If you hear me wrong you're going to sink.

There are going to be times in your life when it's going to feel like all of hell is against you.

And your escape is not just hanging in there and kind of reluctantly try and employ some Scriptural principle, while all the while _'Oh God!'_ and pray for better days.

You have to come against those forces paraded against you,

…you have to come against that severe affliction,

…_you have to come against that thing whatever it is, **with a greater faith than that fear is trying to present you with.**_

When people start ridiculing you, when people start slandering you, (I'm bringing up various things that could come against you as affliction,) _instead of slandering back, **bless**_ _**them**; it's the best way to overcome that affliction._

The moment you come _with that opposite spirit,_ **you neutralize the platform for the enemy to operate from.**

...and I'm now talking about symptoms in your body as well, coming against you as affliction;

...the moment you come with that opposite spirit of faith instead of fear, **you neutralize the platform for the enemy to operate from.**

You destroy his strategy.

When people come to you and they're ugly towards you, and they do mean things, **love them back with extreme measures of love,**

...because you wrestle not against flesh and blood!

So, when the enemy afflicts you with poverty, when he afflicts you with need, **go to the extreme of giving.**

Give according to your means _and beyond,_

BEYOND!

Give motivated by your faith and your abundant joy because of your covenant love relationship with God!

You see we're dealing with a real enemy.

I know he's defeated, **but he will defeat you if you walk in ignorance and in little faith** *concerning your righteousness, concerning the Word of Covenant, and the covenant love of God.*

Discover *the resource* of God's abundance,

Discover *the Greater One that indwells you.*

2Corinthians 9:8

8 *"**God IS able; to make all grace abound towards you,** that you will **always**,* (and always includes the most miserable day you could ever face,) *have enough of everything you need..."*

But what do you have?

What is this *'enough of everything'* that you **have?**

A treasure in the heavenly places, a treasure in the spirit realm of spiritual realities, *of spiritual truth,*

...I'm talking about righteousness, a covenant relationship with God, an intimate love relationship with your Daddy God who cares for you!

God himself is that treasure Paul speaks of in Ephesians 1:3 when he says that,

"God has blessed us with every blessing in the heavenly places."

God has blessed us with Himself, *with everything He could possibly mean to us in Covenant love relationship.*

Sometimes you know, we read that Scripture, and we think, *'Well, what does my heavenly inheritance mean to me when I need $10.00 now?*

"God has blessed me with every spiritual blessing in the heavenly places."

Oh, it's a wonderful thought for this week by and by, but brother, right now I need $10.00'

We need to stop thinking of heavenly places as some kind of area in outer space somewhere or some kind of place like Heaven, you know,

…like only the people, on the other side of the grave, you know, *they've got access into that Heaven, but not me.*

Heavenly places is a realm, *an eternal spirit realm that is more real than the natural realm*

...and your access into that realm is through the birth of faith in your heart!

...and through your understanding of your righteousness and through faith in the Word of God!

...through faith in your love covenant with God!

You no longer need to walk by the visible, by the things that you see, *but you walk by unseen realities.*

And the things God has granted you *are all there in that place, in that unseen realm, in seed form,*

*...***and by faith you plug into the truth of the Word, into the seed of that Word, *and employ that seed into your situation.***

When you are faced with a severe test of affliction, whether it be in any area that the enemy comes against you, either in your health, or in your finances, or someone bringing you into ill repute, **you respond to it with a strong release in your heart, of knowledge, of truth,**

*...*because you've got a heavenly bank account, you've got a heavenly treasure of truth; **you've got a heavenly treasure in your God,**

*…and you've got a treasure in your heart **of every reality of your New Covenant friendship and love relationship with God.***

You know, 2Peter 1 speaks of it, how God has kept in the heavens *these truths that He has now revealed to us in Christ.*

The prophetic Word carried and sustained the promise for years and generations, *but we have now received that inheritance,*

*…*and God *"**desires to show more convincingly** to the heirs of the promise…"*

We are the heirs of the promise,

…but if we don't believe it,

…if we're not convinced,

*…**the promise is of no meaning to us.***

***But God desires to convince us of His own conviction** concerning this covenant love relationship,*

*…***concerning our righteousness,** so that we can draw boldly from it!*

In Proverbs 4 from verse 20 I think, it says that **we've got to *guard* (protect) *the Word* (protect our understanding of the truth) *and treasure it above everything else that have value,***

…and keep our hearts (or guard our hearts with truth, with that eternal truth we value, that eternal truth revealed to us in Christ, we must keep these things) *with all vigilance, for from **it** flow the issues of life.*

The heart carries the seed.

The heart of faith becomes the womb which carries the seed of promise,

…**and God's integrity is in that seed,**

…**God's life is in that seed, His provision is in that seed.**

So when you're faced with a severe test of affliction, don't just hang in there, *come against it!*

I've seen through the years, many believers, just hanging in there, and ten years later *they're still hanging,*

…some of them have been hanged to death, strangled by the circumstance.

Listen, you've got to come against it with a greater aggression, *an aggression of spirit, **an unshakable confidence of heart in your God,***

…***laying boldly ahold of what you have in Christ Jesus,***

This is the victory that overcomes every opposition and every obstacle, <u>even our faith</u>

...it overcomes the world!

...if it's financially,

...give like you've never given before,

...but not reluctantly, or full of fear and anxiety, or feeling obligated,

...but through a faith release,

...through trust in God and love for God,

...give like you've never given before,

...because in your heart, through meditation, and through setting your mind on these truths, these realities, you have discovered that <u>God's measure</u> far out measures your need!

You could never develop a need *that is so big or so unique* **that God can no longer help you.**

2Corinthians 8:3 & 4

3 *"For they gave, according to their means, as I can testify,* **and beyond their means, <u>by their own free will</u>***,"*

215

4 *"...**begging us earnestly, for the favor of taking part in the needs of the saints**..."*

Today we have the reverse of that.

The ministers beg the congregation earnestly, and in every newsletter,

'Oh if you guys don't give, you know, this ministry is going to go down the drain,'

...and so they've gone down the drain, *one after the other!*

But there back in those days when 2Corinthians 8:3 was written, **there was such faith released through the word of righteousness, through the New Covenant in Christ's blood, through the truth of identity and sonship and God's love,** *that the people begged the apostles earnestly for the opportunity to give.*

The people begged the apostles earnestly.

They looked at it as a favor and a privilege to be able to give into someone else's need!

Would you agree that *that's giving cheerfully not reluctantly or under obligation?*

Hallelujah!

2Corinthians 8:3-5

3 *"For they gave, according to their means, as I can testify,* **and beyond their means, <u>by their own free will</u>***,"*

4 *"...***begging us earnestly, for the favor of taking part in the needs of the saints***"*

5 *"...***and this they did,** *beyond our expectation;* **they first gave themselves to the Lord, by the will of God, and then to us also.***"*

Listen God wants you in ministry, *to minister out of the abundance of the heart!*

...**out of that** *overflow,*

...*to give with such abundance of that* <u>*wealth*</u> *that you walk in,*

...*of that wealth that's within you!*

...**of that righteousness** *that you enjoy,*

...**so that you'll never ever need to hint for money!**

There will be times that you'll face temporal needs, like when Jesus sat at the well, *conscious of his thirst, of his hunger, of the weariness of his body* ...but then the women arrived, *and he began to minister to her* **out of the wealth of His spirit**.

She still wanted to talk religion and politics, *'I'm a Samaritan and you're a Jew and we don't have any dealings with each other,'*

…because she wasn't going to just give him water, she was either going to sell it to him; or she was going to take full advantage of him and exploit his need in some way or the other.

But Jesus says,

'Hey if you knew who it was that is speaking to you…'

He knew He was more than a Jew,

*…**He knew that He was more than just a natural man** being thirsty right now, being hungry right now, being tired right now,*

*…**He knew He was speaking for the Father.***

And you will overcome your temporal needs *on that same principle.*

Don't ever allow your consciousness of need now *to overrule the reality of who you are in Christ Jesus.*

We need to discover that our identity in Christ is much more than what we are in the natural,

…so that when you're faced with a situation like Jesus was faced with at the well,

…instead of allowing himself to communicate on her level,

…on the level of, you know, 'You're a Samaritan, I'm a Jew, I'm thirsty, don't worry about politics woman, we can sort that out later, I've got other guys, twelve of them, they've gone to buy food, they've got money, and when they come back we'll pay you for the water.'

No,

He was more sensitive to the Holy Spirit, than his own temporal needs,

…and as he started sharing out of the wealth in his spirit, <u>his temporal need got taken care of</u>

…and he ended up reaching a whole city with the Gospel.

I say again, God wants you in ministry *to give with such abundance, out of the wealth of righteousness*,

…*to give out of the wealth* of that covenant relationship of love that you walk in

…*that you'll never ever need to hint for money!*

In closing, I urge you to get yourself a copy of *"The Mirror Bible"* available online at:

www.friendsofthemirror.com or at www.amazon.com and several other book sellers.

If you want me or someone a part of our team to come to where you are, anywhere in the world, and give a talk, or teach you and some of your friends about the gospel message, and redemption truths and realities, simply contact us at www.livingwordintl.com …or you can always find me on www.facebook.com

If you have been helped, or your perspective on life and ministry has changed as a result of reading this book, please get in touch with me and let me know.

I would love to share your joy,

…so that my joy in writing this book *may be full!*

That which was from the beginning,

which we have heard
(with our spiritual ears),
which we have seen
(with our spiritual eyes),
which we have looked upon
(beheld, focused our attention
upon),
and which our hands have also
handled
(which we have also
experienced),

concerning the Word of life,

we declare to you,

that you also may have this
fellowship with us;

and truly our fellowship is with
the Father
and with His Son Jesus Christ.

And these things we write to you
that your joy may be full.

~ 1John 1:1-4

About the Author

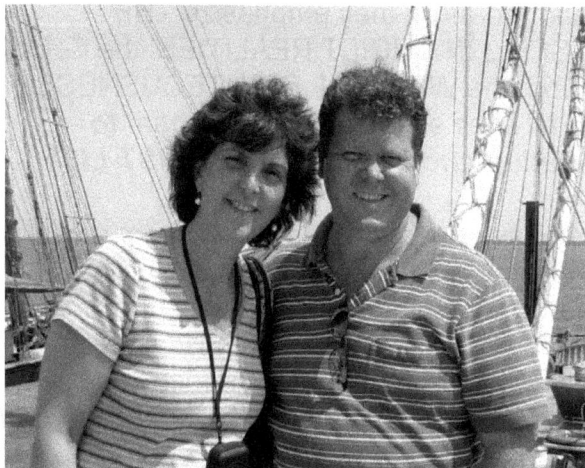

Rudi & Carmen Louw together oversee and pastor a church: Living Word International. They also travel and minister both locally and internationally.

Rudi was born and raised in the country of South Africa, while Carmen grew up in Cortland, New York.

They function in the ministry of reconciliation (2Corinthians 5:18-21) and flow strongly in the gifts of the Holy Spirit and His anointing to teach, preach, prophecy, heal *and whatever is needed to touch people's lives with the reality of God's love and power.*

God has given them keen insight into what He has to say to mankind in the work of redemption, concerning the revelation of, and restoration of, *humanity's true identity,*

…and therefore they emphasize THE GOSPEL; IN CHRIST REALITIES; the GRACE of God; the WORD OF RIGHTEOUSNESS, *and all such eternal truths **essential to salvation and living of the CHRIST-LIFE***

They have been granted this wisdom and revelation into the knowledge of God by the resurrected Spirit of Jesus Christ, the Holy Spirit of Truth sent down from Heaven, proceeding from the Father Himself, *to establish and strengthen believers **in the faith of God, and to activate them in ministering to others.***

Not only are people set free from the poison and bondage of sin, condemnation and all kinds of intimidation, (upheld, strengthened and reinforced by age old religious ideas born out of ignorance,) but many are brought into a closer more intimate relationship with Father God, **as Daddy,** through accurate teaching, and unveiling of the gospel message, prophetic words, healings and miracles.

Rudi & Carmen are closely knitted together with many other effective Christians, church fellowships, and groups of believers who share the same revelation and passion.

www.ingramcontent.com/pod-product-compliance
Lightning Source LLC
Chambersburg PA
CBHW051823090426
42736CB00011B/1617